By F
with

M000079591

In Lieu of Flowers,
God Gave Us a Miracle
The True-Life Story Of Zach Sandy

WhiteStone Publishing
Stonewood, WV, USA

In Lieu of Flowers, God Gave Us A Miracle

ISBN-10: 162883000X

ISBN-13: 978-1-62883-000-2

Library of Congress Control Number: 2013942876

Printed in the United States of America.

This book may be purchased online at:

http://whitestonepublishing.com

http://authorstock.com/zach

http://amazon.com

and other fine retailers.

Bookstores, distributors, pastors, and churches may purchase this book in bulk. For details & contact information, visit:

http://whitestonepublishing.com/books/zach

WHITESTONE
PUBLISHING
CHRISTIAN RESOURCES | INSPIRATIONAL NOVELS | CHILDREN'S BOOKS

Table of Contents

Chapter 1: Struggle From the Start.............................1

Chapter 2: Dedicated From the Start.........................7

Chapter 3: Middle School and High School.............13

Chapter 4: Prelude to a Miracle 19

Chapter 5: Disaster Strikes..23

Chapter 6: The Beginning of a Miracle 37

Chapter 7: Valley of the Shadow of Death...............47

Chapter 8: In the Land of a Thousand Questions.....67

Chapter 9: The Great Awakening..............................75

Chapter 10: The Long Way Home (Miracle Road)... 83

Chapter 11: Coming Home 105

Chapter 12: The Sky is the Limit............................135

Appendix: Testimonials...141

Chapter 1:
Struggle From the Start

In March of 1994 Cheri Sandy had carried our second child for eight and a half months, and she was tiring out, which is not unusual at that stage. The eighth month seemed to take forever. It was still very cold in March that year; winter did not want to give way to spring just yet. My brother, John, and I customarily attended the annual West Virginia Boys High School Basketball Tournament in the Civic Center in Charleston, WV (about 120 miles from our home in Stonewood, WV). Plans were made to attend again that year. The tournaments ran Wednesday through Saturday. Cheri and I discussed the possibility of the baby coming while I was at the tournaments. Cheri did not want me to go. Several family members were secured to be ready to help if needed, and a few nights someone stayed with her to make her feel at ease. I used the hotel phone to communicate with Cheri in the mornings, afternoons, and evenings. (Not everyone had cell phones back then.)

Friday evening around 5:30 PM, John and I were sitting at the Civic Center watching a basketball game, when, during a break in the action, the intercom rang out "Russell Sandy, report to the announcer's table." (How did we ever communicate without cell phones?) As we approached the announcer's table, I wondered of the possible messages I would receive. The gentleman there handed me a note that read simply, "Baby is coming!!!" There was no further information. We had no way to get any more information prior to arrival at the United Hospital Center in Clarksburg, WV—about two-plus hours away—unless we stopped at a pay phone and called the hospital. Now, it did not take us quite that long to get there. (I can't say exactly how long—I might incriminate myself.) I believe we did have to stop and put fuel in the vehicle. Once we arrived at the hospital we were directed to the maternity floor, where we found family members and saw the baby through the windows. Cheri was still in recovery.

We soon learned about the events that had preceded that moment. I felt bad because one of the possibilities that we previously discussed had unfortunately taken place. Cheri actually hemorrhaged while she was at home with Tracy Sandy, Rhonda DeMoss, and Rusty and Felicia Sandy.

Cheri's hemorrhaging had launched everyone into high gear. Tracy (sister-in-law) had made a lot of phone calls to the doctor's office and to 911. She also alerted family members. Once those calls went out, the phone had rung back in. It was Robert and the late Ada "Nanny" Wright calling to see if they needed to come and get the kids to take them to their house. In due time they did. In the meantime, when the ambulance arrived at the house everyone was pleased to see that Mark and Meredith McClain, a husband-wife team that attended our church and were personal friends, were staffing it.

They found that Cheri's water had broken in addition to the bleeding. She was rushed to United Hospital Center in Clarksburg, WV, where Dr. Gyimesi was waiting for her in the operating room. He had previously scheduled Cheri for a C-Section, which was to take place 11 days later, had she been able to go that long. (That plan was due to a complication that he had detected, called placenta previa.) Tracy rode along with Cheri in the ambulance. At the hospital other family members were waiting.

There had been some very anxious moments, but eventually Zachary Patrick Sandy had arrived. From the start, he had difficulty breathing on his own. He was placed inside an incubator, and he was connected to a machine that helped him breathe, as well as having a feeding tube inserted via his nose. We were not permitted to hold our newborn for the first time until two to three days later. There was much prayer! For this tiny fighter, "struggle" seemed to be a way of life from the beginning. We had no way to know the degree of insurmountable odds that Zach would eventually overcome—thanks to having the Lord Jesus Christ on his side.

Zach was a *miracle baby* because of what he went through during the birthing process.

"Before I formed thee in the belly I knew thee; and before thou camest forth out of the womb I sanctified thee" *(Jeremiah 1:5).*

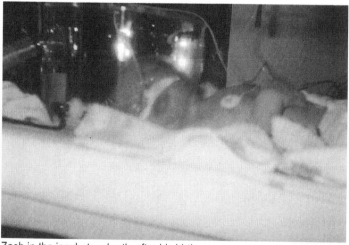

Zach in the incubator shortly after his birth.

From left to right: Zach Sandy, Samuel Vaughn, and Brandon Sandy with their grandfather, Papaw Russell Sandy. These three cousins bonded early in a tight friendship that has lasted through triumphs and tragedy. More about these three coming up!

Chapter 2:
Dedicated From the Start

Zachary Patrick Sandy was a happy baby, loved by all, and spoiled by most. Zach had an older brother, Russell Benjamen, who was proud of his little brother and instantly relished the role of "older brother." At two weeks old, Zach was dedicated to the Lord Jesus Christ in a ceremony held at our church, the House of the Lord Jesus Christ in Clarksburg, WV, then pastored by his Papaw, the late Russell F. Sandy. Unlike other babies, Zach didn't cry very much. Cheri was an awesome Mom, and she had help from family to babysit, so she could work. Zach's Dad (wow, I was called that even back then?) held down various jobs and still the family struggled some, as so many families do. Yet we seemed to always have good Christmas times and good birthdays for both boys.

Zach grew up wearing some of his older brother's hand-me-down clothes. When Zach was around nine or ten years old, he suddenly changed his whole outlook on what type of clothes he wanted to wear. Air Jordan, Nike, Under Armour, etc.—nothing else would do. Cheri and I struggled to find these brands at the local Goodwill stores or on sale in outlet stores, and we were quite successful. Very few times did we pay the ballooned prices for brand names.

Zach was active in youth sports. Baseball and football were his favorites. He had several coaches that made a positive impact in his life. There were too many to name them all. Baseball seemed to be his favorite sport.

Just as soon as our sons could barely fit a glove on their hand, I tossed ball with each of them. Some of our fondest memories were made those days. Rusty tried so hard to like sports—he wanted to make his Dad proud. He did well, but you could tell his heart just wasn't in it. Rusty came to me one day in the middle of a game at Nutter Fort Park and said, "Dad, I don't want to play anymore." His wish was granted. Rusty was going to be a preacher, and his Mom and I were very proud of that.

Zach continued to play ball, meet new friends, and have fun. Along the way, his basketball coaches and football coaches gave him nicknames such as Marshmallow, Hollywood, and Sparkplug. Zach played in several baseball leagues, including some all-star competitions. He also played with a "travel baseball team" coached by Todd Kiger, a coach that Zach says taught him the most about baseball. Zach played some basketball in

Jerry West leagues in his hometown. He played football from the time he could hold one until he graduated from high school.

After the passing of Papaw Sandy, our family eventually began attending Christian Apostolic Church in Clarksburg, under Pastor Terry Null (and later Pastor Doug Joseph). It was there that Zach, at eight years of age, knelt at an altar of prayer and repented (turned to God and away from the world). While his uncle, John Sandy, was praying with him that night, Zach was filled with the Holy Ghost—God came into his soul and Zach spoke in heavenly tongues (the initial, physical evidence of the baptism of the Holy Ghost). That same night his cousin, Tiffany Sandy, was also filled with the Holy Ghost with the evidence of speaking with other tongues as the Spirit gave the utterance.

Soon afterward both were water baptized (by John Sandy) in the wonderful name of the Lord Jesus Christ. Zach's mother, Cheri, was always active in the church. Sadly, at that time I was not fully consistent in serving the Lord, but as parents we always stressed that sports and extracurricular activities were never as important as a personal relationship with God. Many family nights were devoted to Bible study and prayer. Zach's older brother, Rusty, had been studying to be a preacher. Cheri and I could see the same in Zach. When he was 13 years old, after attending a church summer camp,

Zach told us that he was feeling a call from the Lord upon his life regarding ministry.

Over time several preachers mentioned to us that they sensed a confirmation of Zach's calling. On several occasions, as the four of us talked about the Bible during times of devotion in the evenings, Rusty and Zach both took turns having a scripture to discuss. Eventually they did more than just read a scripture. They would practically preach a sermon to Mom and Dad.

Eventually I got serious about church. The Bible says, "Choose you this day whom ye will serve" (Joshua 24:15). It was the best decision of my life to live for God. In my home I am well known for this quote: "It is a good life living for the Lord." Cheri and I were so proud of our boys for how they were growing up in the church and because both had a burden to do what they could for the kingdom of God. Rusty had preached a few times already, including preaching in other churches.

On Easter Sunday, 2008, at Christian Apostolic Church, Zach stood behind the pulpit for the very first time. He was very nervous, but it helped a lot that he had led devotions at times in our home. Rusty and Zach preached—Zach first, then Rusty. Cheri and I were so proud that day. The title of Zach's message was "How Strong Is Your Hedge?" His selected text was in

Mark 11. Zach asked the church, "How strong is the hedge around you, that keeps out temptation and worldly lusts?" The message did not take long—about 10 minutes—but something had begun. Zach was going to be a preacher.

Chapter 3:
Middle School and High School

et's backtrack for some details about school and sports. Rusty had gone to Bridgeport High School (crosstown rival of Robert C. Byrd High School in Clarksburg). Zach was ready for sixth grade. When football practice time came around, Zach went to the first practice, ready to play football for Bridgeport Middle School. That would eventually lead to playing for Bridgeport High School's football program, which is one of the finest in the state. They had won many state championships.

Zach went to his first "team lift," where the football team gathers and lifts weights, working out with the help of the coaches. Zach was not happy when he came home that day. Cheri and I tried to find out what was wrong. After a couple hours of Zach being unusually quiet and staying off to himself, he finally opened up to us about the matter.

Zach said, "There are boys in the weight room lifting 200 and 300 pounds. I can't even lift the barbell that the weights go on. Several of the boys thought that was funny. I am just not going back there."

Cheri and I sat down with him and tried to help him deal with the disappointment.

I told Zach, "There are two ways to go from here. One, you can quit, give up, and back down from the challenge that is presented to you. Or, two, you can decide that you are a fighter and determine to obtain the goal that you set for yourself."

Cheri and I decided to get a small weight bench for the boys. Zach went to lifting for the workouts and waited until everyone else was done to lift on his own with a few friends. Zach really worked hard at home. To this day I can remember hearing the weights clanging in the next room. Zach didn't get to play much in middle school.

While he was playing freshman football at Bridgeport High School, the team went undefeated, beating teams by three to four touchdowns. The last game of his freshman year was against the team of Robert C. Byrd High School, their crosstown rival.

The rival team had kids that Zach knew well. He had gone to grade school with them. He knew practically all of them. Bridgeport scored early and often. Zach got to play tailback in the second half. He ran the ball several times, actually scoring a touchdown in the early part of the fourth quarter—making the score 40 to zero.

Zach then transferred back to RCB for his sophomore year, because driving six miles to school at Bridgeport every day, and then to practices, was going to be too much. Zach had a blast his first two years at RCB. He met lots of new friends. Zach's senior year of high school began with great expectations. Football practice started it off. Zach figured to play a lot that year; he had worked hard in the off-season on his bench press, speed, and agility. Every day he would be at the field house, lifting and working out. Football season was successful. The team's record was six and four (6-4).

Zach played a key role in the team's final regular season game. Robert C. Byrd High was playing Lewis County High. If RCB lost, there would be no playoffs for the team that year. Late in the fourth quarter, during a rainy, muddy night at RCB's football field, the home team held a slim lead as Lewis County marched down the field to what was shaping up as an apparent victory for the visitors.

With LCH having possession deep in the RCB Eagles' territory, the opposing team was driving for the go-ahead score. The quarterback for Lewis County handed the ball off to their running back. As he came through

the line, one of the RCB linebackers caused him to
fumble, and Zach pounced on the loose football. That
turnover, a recovered fumble, was the end of LCH's
drive. The game ended with RCB still ahead. The
Eagles made the playoffs. They lost in the first round of
the playoffs, though, and football was over.

Zach worked hard on academics and carried a grade
point average of 3.5 during the school year. A few times
during the year, classmates decorated Zach's car (a
black, 2000 Dodge Neon). At one point Zach even
painted the car's rims with RCB's school colors, green
and blue, before he settled on all black.

Baseball season quickly came. Practice seemed to take
forever, and then the team waited on good weather. I
remember that on opening night the game was in
Buckhannon, WV. The team stretched and went
through warm-ups. When the starting lineups were
announced, there was a good feeling because Zach had
earned a starting position in right field.

RCB played a few games before they made a planned
trip to Myrtle Beach to play teams from other states, to
find good weather, and to just plain have a vacation.
The baseball season went OK—around .500 overall.
Zach didn't set any records at the plate for RCB, but he
was a jewel in the field, with several outstanding
catches—and he was always a spark plug in the dugout,

trying to fire the team up. Soon baseball was over and it was time for graduation.

Zach's Papaw Welch was one of the ministers asked to say a few words at the baccalaureate. At the graduation, many family members were in attendance, as was Rev. Doug Joseph (his pastor since 2002). Zach had several pictures taken with friends, family, and members of the baseball teams. One memorable picture from that night showed Zach with his hands raised in a manner that signified being *victorious*. Little did we know that the image foretold a huge miracle in his life, prophesying victory over a terrible tragedy just a few months ahead.

Zach's graduation from Robert C. Byrd High School, May 25, 2012

A graduation party was held in honor of Zach and two of his cousins that graduated the same year: Samuel Vaughn of Watkinsville, Georgia, and Brandon Sandy of Martinsburg, WV. The three of them were the same age, and they had grown up together. When they graduated together, the three families reunited to celebrate at Clarksburg City Park in Nutter Fort, WV. Plans were made that day for the three cousins to attend the church summer camp (as they had done several years in the past) to be held in a few weeks near Charleston, WV.

Chapter 4:
Prelude to a Miracle

Now that high school was behind Zach, he set his sights on the future and began job hunting. He had worked in fast food restaurants during school, whenever he could. Zach put in several applications and hoped for the best.

Zach sent a text message to a friend from the past, Cayla Bayles, daughter of Rev. Dan Bayles, pastor of Calvary Apostolic Church in Uniontown, PA. Plans were made to meet at the local mall just to hang out.

Around that time, Zach had secured a job at United Hospital Center in Bridgeport, WV. Zach actually went to two days of job orientation and was ready to start work. His first shift was set to be on July 12, 2012—the Thursday after he was to return from the church summer camp.

Among all else that was going on, the Sandy family had also planned our annual trip to Ocean City around July 4, for the Independence Day holiday. We had visited Ocean City almost every year since Zach was a baby, missing only a few years. Fishing, relaxing, shopping, and good food were always the attractions of Ocean City, and there was the Sandy's favorite hotel. The Plim Plaza Hotel is the only place we stayed during all the years we have visited Ocean City.

We made our July 4 trip. It was a good week, weather wise, and the fireworks at the beach never disappoint. Cheri and I were able to relax. We felt rested and ready for whatever work and life had to offer us that summer.... If we only knew that in just a few days our world would be turned upside down, and then we would sit back and watch our great, big, awesome God perform mighty acts right in front of our eyes.

Saturday, our vacation was nearing an end. We made our way back towards West Virginia. As we drove back, we stopped in Martinsburg, WV, to pick up Brandon Sandy, so that Brandon and Zach, along with Samuel Vaughn, could go to the youth camp in Charleston.

We decided to go to Washington, PA, on Saturday night and get a hotel room, just to prolong vacation one more day. Our thinking was that once Zach started his job that next Thursday, there would be very little chance that we as a family would be able to schedule a vacation together the rest of the year. Zach and Brandon had a blast. On Sunday morning we all headed to Stonewood, WV.

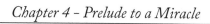

Chapter 5:
Disaster Strikes

During the week while we were in Ocean City, there had been strong storms across a broad area of the United States, including West Virginia. An AccuWeather.com headline for July 2, 2012 said, "Intense Storms Called a 'Derecho' Slam 700 Miles of the US." The article's lead paragraph stated:

> A "super derecho" of violent thunderstorms left a more than 700-mile trail of destruction across the Midwest and mid-Atlantic on Friday, cutting power to millions and killing thirteen people.

Right: A once-tidy fireworks tent operated by our church was utterly destroyed by the Derecho-class storm front. Hundreds of such tents were knocked down across the storms' wide path.

Power was out in many cities, and it was slow getting the power back on in several places. Sunday and Monday there were worries that the church youth camp would have to be moved back at least a day. Then word came from the WV District of the United Pentecostal Church International (the church group sponsoring the event) that the UPCI youth camp was going to have to be cancelled, because no electrical power was available at the venue site. All three boys were down in the dumps, because it was their last bit of freedom together before college and work.

Then Brandon and Samuel got a call from a close friend in Summersville, WV, inviting them to attend a different UPCI youth camp with them in Virginia. Zach was not going to be able to go, because of starting his new job on Thursday.

The two cousins were picked up later that night and journeyed to the Virginia campground the next day. Of course, Zach was down because he didn't get to attend camp with his cousins one last time together. Apparently there was not going to be any church camp for Zach that year.

Sometime on Tuesday afternoon, Zach received a phone call from his aunt, Susan Moran, inviting him to attend a church camp at Parkersburg, WV, that was sponsored by a sister organization, the Assemblies of the Lord Jesus Christ. She picked him up on Tuesday evening to attend that night's service at the ALJC youth camp. Zach came home late that night very excited about the services. He asked Cheri and I if he could go back the next day and spend all day with his cousin, Jesse Glaspell. Cheri and I were relieved that Zach was going to get to be in church camp after all. We knew that it was very important to him.

Above: Spreading Truth Ministries, site of the ALJC youth camp.

Early the next morning, on July 11, 2012, Zach received a phone call from my cousin, Brad Glaspell, and they made plans for Brad to pick up Zach at our house around 8:00 AM to make the trip to Parkersburg. Zach was excited to make the most of his last day before starting his new job. He was also excited to spend some time with his cousin, Jesse, and to meet new friends. Cheri and I had never met anyone from this church camp, but we maintain complete trust in the good judgment of our relatives, Susan Moran and Brad Glaspell.

Brad kept some preaching CDs in the vehicle. During the drive over, they listened to some parts of a sermon in which the preacher spoke about miracles. Brad testified that Zach opened up to him a little during the drive about wanting to do more for the kingdom of God.

At around 10:11 AM, Zach sent me a text message confirming that they had arrived in Parkersburg at the campground. Out of respect, Zach often sent text messages to either his Mom or to me, letting us know his whereabouts, so we would not worry about him.

Brad and Zach walked into the morning church service as the preacher was finishing his sermon. The minister mentioned miracles in his message.

The minister asked all the youth to come forward to pray. There was an awesome worship atmosphere. Pastor Ralph Tisdale, superintendent of the WV District ALJC and leader of the host

Pastor Ralph Tisdale,
Superintendent, WV District ALJC

church, came to the microphone and asked for everyone's attention. He directed everyone in the crowd to ask God for three miracles in each of their lives: one for your church, another for your family, and a third for yourself.

This may seem like a simple prayer, but later, after the accident, Zach explained the three miracles that he asked for that morning. For his church, Zach asked for unity and that the church would grow. He then asked for his family to become stronger and see each other more. Then for himself, Zach prayed for a greater testimony. He said that ever since he was young he had always been taught to tell people what God has done for you, if you want them to come to church. So he asked that God would give him a testimony that would blow people's minds. Zach could not have imagined that in just a few hours, a miracle of epic proportions would begin, right down on the softball field. (Cheri and I now joke that if Zach ever desires anything he is to run it past us before he actually asks for it.)

The service was over soon after. There were many events scheduled in which the youth could participate. There was a scavenger hunt and a hotdog-eating contest. Zach was having a good time with his cousin, Jesse Glaspell. They heard that there was a softball game about to start down on the field, so the two cousins headed down to join in.

Upon arriving at the softball field, Caleb Tisdale introduced himself to Zach. It was the first time that Zach Sandy and Caleb Tisdale had met. Who could know at that moment how significant a role Caleb would play in Zach's life within just a few minutes?

Rev. Caleb Tisdale, WV ALJC, son of Pastor Ralph Tisdale.

The softball field at Spreading Truth Ministries in Parkersburg, WV.

All shook hands, and they agreed, "Let's play ball!" Weather wise, it was good day. There were very few clouds. The forecast called for sunshine and a very slim chance of rain.

At 2:28 PM Zach sent a text message to my phone that simply said, "Playing softball." To this very day, I have the text saved on my phone. The game began, and the first batter was Zach's cousin, Jesse. He hit a triple. Zach was in leftfield, and his cousin was on third base. Jesse

turned and started joking with Zach. The two were laughing. As Jesse turned, Caleb had just released the first pitch to the next batter.

Suddenly there was a loud bang. Caleb described it as a "bomb" going off.

It had to have happened between 2:28 and 2:44 PM. 2:28 is when Zach had sent the text message to me, and 2:44 is when Brad Glaspell called me with the news of what had happened.

The camp evangelist, Michael Jadrnicek, later said, "I was on the hill overlooking the softball field, and I saw a huge bolt of lightning hit that young man on the head."

Pastor Ralph Tisdale's wife was on third base, and she later remarked, "I felt like I was hit on the back of the head with a softball."

Paramedic Jim Lemley and partner Shawn McKenna, who were a few miles away in Vienna, WV, saw the bolt of lightning, and Jim remarked, "That was a weird lightning strike. I bet we get a call on that one."

The fulfillment of that rather prophetic statement came within about thirty seconds or so. A call came in that a child had been struck by lightning at Spreading Truth Ministries on Earl Core Road in Parkersburg.

Lightning had struck Zach Sandy on the top of his head, leaving an entrance wound in the form of singed hair and a small "incision" mark outlined in red. The lightning traveled through his head and body, burning him and leaving other evidences, including broad "track marks" of a deep purple/red color on his right arm, down his side, and down the center of his back. (It was as though it caused an instant micro boiling of the blood in his capillaries along the paths chosen by the lightning.) He had burns that had manifested practically instantly.

The lightning exited his feet both from the bottoms (soles) and on the outward facing edges (along the "blade") of each foot, just above the soles of his shoes, about midway between the heel and toe. Both of his socks and both shoes had corresponding holes punched by the lightning as it found its way out. The holes were about a quarter of an inch in diameter.

Zach's body instantly stiffened and went to the ground. He was not breathing, and he had no pulse (no heartbeat). Zach was dead.

Caleb Tisdale (at the pitcher's mound) was knocked down by the impact of the strike. He picked himself up from the ground and looked about. He was trying to figure out what just happened. As he gathered himself, he turned to see folks running toward the gymnasium, which was located up the hill some distance from the ball field.

Caleb's father, Pastor Ralph Tisdale, was in centerfield. He also was knocked down during the strike. He had been talking on his cellphone to Brother Jim Workman at the moment the bolt hit. Just as his son was doing, Pastor Tisdale gathered himself, trying to figure out what had just taken place. He quickly placed his cellphone into his shirt pocket—without turning it off. Thus, Jim Workman heard an audio accounting of all that happened over the few minutes that followed.

Pastor Ralph Tisdale was trying to help everyone move toward the gymnasium as he met up with Caleb, just in time to hear Caleb say, "Oh, Lord!"

Caleb had spotted Zach—motionless, not responding to the call for "everyone to get to the gym." Caleb later testified that as he approached Zach's lifeless body, it was the ugliest site that he had ever seen.

Ralph Tisdale handed his phone to his wife and pleaded, *"Call 911 right now!"*

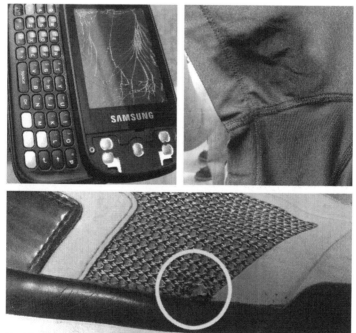

Zach's phone was destroyed, clothes burned and melted, shoes pierced.

There were several calls to 911 in the next few minutes. Caleb quickly began to assess the situation. (Later he described Zach's appearance.) Zach was stiff as a board. Smoke was coming from Zach's mouth. His clothes were half blown off of him. His hair was singed and sticking straight up. His eyes were open, but rolled back in his head. His ears and lips were black from the lightning and blue from the lack of oxygen. The lightning had boiled the sweat on his arms. Caleb said that Zach looked and smelled like he had been in a fire.

Zach's cell had a shattered screen, covers blown off, and buttons melted.

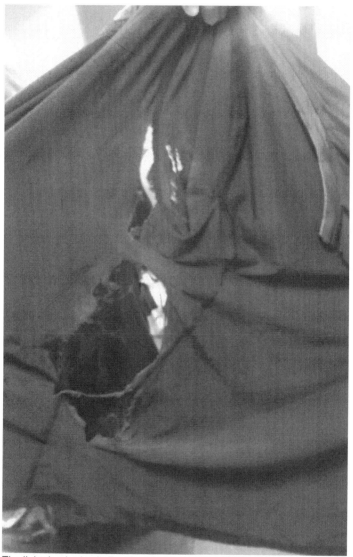

The lightning had split Zach's shirt (shown here) and pants nearly in two.

Caleb Tisdale took off his own shirt to put over Zach's mouth, and he began CPR. Caleb is a certified lifeguard. Although he had his CPR certification, he had never done CPR on a human being (only on practice mannequins). Caleb administered breaths to Zach, and then he prayed in tongues while he did chest compressions. Caleb later said, "When you do not have the words, you just talk with God." Ralph Tisdale held Zach's head and prayed, also speaking with tongues, while checking from time to time to see if there was any response from Zach's lifeless body. The elder Tisdale took note that around Zach's ears and mouth, the blueness would grow fainter when the compressions were done. Although the skin never returned to the normal color it should be, it seemed clear that the CPR was helping.

Lindsay Leasure-Kupfner and her mother, Sandy, heard the call go out over the scanner. They both rushed to their car and drove to the church campgrounds to see if they could help. Sandy's mom runs a daycare in Parkersburg—and they thought the original call said an 8-year-old child had been struck by lightning. (The difference between "18" and "8" is an understandable mistake, granting the tension of the situation.) Lindsay helped with CPR until the ambulance came.

Many saints around the scene, including Brad Glaspell, were praying diligently for God to intervene for Zach.

Prayer changes things! *Prayer changes things!*

Chapter 6:
The Beginning of a Miracle

Brad has testified that he did not want to call Zach's dad with the news. It was 2:44 PM when Brad called. I was at home. I had just finished a work shift from 4:30 AM to 1:00 PM at United Hospital Center in Bridgeport, WV (which is in the Clarksburg area). I would routinely stop on the way home from work to see my wife at her workplace, sometimes bringing her some lunch. That day I stopped in and spent a few minutes with her, and then I went home to take a nap, which was typical after a morning shift. I had just lain down, not ten minutes before, when the phone rang.

There were times when I would turn my phone off so I could rest. I am thankful I did not this time. I noticed Brad's phone number on my caller-ID screen, but I could never have guessed how much this call would change my life forever. Brad was sobbing so deeply that it took a couple of times of him repeating himself before I knew what he was saying. Zach had been struck by lightning and he was not responding. Brad apologized over and over during the call.

I was so stunned by the news that I cannot remember all of the conversation. However, I do remember that I begged Brad to *tell them to not stop resuscitation under any circumstances*. I reassured Brad that it was not his fault, and I had him explain what happened again. Afterward I told Brad that I had to tell my wife and Rusty, my eldest son, what had happened, and then we would begin the trip to Parkersburg.

When I hung up the phone, I was utterly numb. I felt like I was just punched in the gut and I wanted to throw up. It was like the feeling you have when you wake up from that "really real" dream and you are so stunned because it was just a dream—but this was no dream.

My world had just stopped for a second. I knew that when I informed my other family members their world would also stop for a moment. I raised my head to heaven and talked to God. I had never had to pray with that much fervency in my entire life. I even asked for strength, because I knew that I had to inform the family about what just took place. I had to tell my wife that our youngest son was dead. I had to tell Rusty that his little brother was dead.

Suddenly I could recount every sermon that I had ever heard in my life and every Bible verse I had ever read or heard preached.

"God is our refuge and strength, a very present help in trouble" (Psalm 46:1).

"The name of the Lord is a strong tower: the righteous runneth into it, and is safe" (Proverbs 18:10).

"I will never leave you, nor forsake you" (Hebrews 13:5).

"The Lord is my shepherd; I shall not want" (Psalm 23:1).

"Come unto me, all ye that labour and are heavy laden, and I will give you rest" (Matthew 11:28).

At that moment, more than ever before, I trusted that *prayer changes things.* I prayed, "Lord, my wife and I possess very few things. We are so proud of our boys. Please, please don't take Zach. Please!"

I quickly pulled on clothing and shoes, and I ran to the car, forgetting my reading glasses. I was about to call my wife, but then I thought that I had best wait and tell her face-to-face. I raced to Town & Country Drug Store where she works, about one mile away from our home. I remember that I tried to make a call to Rusty during that trip, but I got no answer (he had worked some overtime).

I arrived at my wife's workplace a minute later, and I parked in front of the store. I hurried inside, and as soon as I went through the front door I made eye contact with her in the back of the store. I was stunned, heartbroken, terrified, and horrified. I wondered if my son was going to make it. I knew that all of the emotions I was feeling, within a few seconds my wife would be feeling the same, as soon as I gave her possibly the worst news she had ever received in her life.

Cheri has a habit of immediately saying, "What's wrong?" whenever she sees someone or when I call her on the phone. As soon as we made eye contact, I knew that she could see the absolute horror in my eyes.

Again she asked, "What's wrong?" but this time when she said it her shoulders seemed to slump and she began to walk quickly toward me.

Cheri knew that something was terribly wrong. I motioned for her and everyone in the pharmacy to come to an office next to the pharmacy.

Cheri repeated, "What's wrong?" several times. The question grew louder and more demanding each time she asked. I put my arm around her and waited until we got in the office together before I told her what had happened. I knew she would break down, as I did when I was informed.

I told her, "Zach has been struck by lightning while playing softball at the camp he went to, and right now he is not responding."

Cheri instantly cried out, "My baby!" and got that look of horror and disbelief as I thought she would. Immediately we knew we had to pray. Our prayer lasted only a few short minutes.

"And this is the confidence that we have in him, that, if we ask any thing according to his will, he heareth us" (I John 5:14).

Nora Harris and Jackie Snider stayed with Cheri to help her phone family and church folks. John Sandy was thought to be the nearest relative to contact, but we thought he was probably asleep, because he works midnight shift and sleeps during the day. Phone calls were unanswered, so it was decided that Jackie would drive to John's house (about a mile away) and try to wake him.

Cheri made several phone calls, and Nora proceeded to call Zach's Nana and Papaw Welch. I had to go outside to get some air. I called Rusty's number, but again I didn't get an answer.

I tried to think, *who can get here the fastest to help me with Cheri?* Cheryl Colombo's number was in my phone. I called her, and amazingly she was just across the bridge from Town & Country. *Thank you, Jesus!* I asked her to please get there quickly, and I told her what had happened. Within 30 seconds she pulled up, and I told her where Cheri was.

I remember calling my sister, Susan Moran. She was at work. We cried together for a minute until she began to firmly assure me that "God can do this!" I agreed and told her that we were getting ready to head to Parkersburg.

I had to get ahold of my brother-in-law, Ashley Vaughn, as well, because Zach's Mamaw (my mother, Helen Sandy) and his cousin, JT Sandy, had been vacationing in Georgia with the Vaughn family. I knew that Zach's situation would soon be listed as a prayer request all over Facebook.com, and that Mamaw Sandy was at the Vaughn residence with only JT Sandy and Landon Vaughn. I did not want to call my Mom when no adult was there to help her deal with the news.

I did get a hold of Ashley, but he was an hour away from the house. Thus I had to pray that he could get home before my Mom heard about it via Facebook, while continuing to believe that God was going to raise Zach. Before I hung up with Ashley, he spoke this scripture to me:

"And ye are complete in Him, which is the head of all principality and power" (Colossians 2:10).

I said, "Zach will be completely healed."

I got a hold of Hannah Sandy (wife of my son, Rusty) and told her to get a hold of Rusty and meet us at Town & Country Drug Store. Rusty called me a few minutes later. Rusty spoke words of faith to me even as I heard his voice tremble.

As Rusty began to say a prayer and reach out for heaven to perform a miracle, I just knew that God heard his prayer. I told Rusty that I had prayed for God to please take me instead.

I had prayed and told the Lord, "I am getting old, and I have diabetes. God, please spare Zach. Take me instead."

Rusty scolded me, saying that God is going to be with Zach, and He will be with us also. Rusty and Zach have always had a special bond that some brothers do not have.

Nora had asked Cheri's Mom and Dad to meet us at Town & Country as well.

My brother, John, called me and asked, "What is going on?"

Jackie had woke him from a deep sleep, and he was headed to Town & Country to be with us.

He pulled up just a minute later and said, "Get in."

I sent Cheryl inside to get Cheri, and within just a few minutes we were off to Parkersburg in the back of John's car.

I phoned Brad Glaspell back, and when he answered I begged him, "Give me some good news."

He did not have good news. Two ambulances and sets of EMTs had arrived, and they were still working on Zach with no response yet. I hung up to make more phone calls. Rusty and Nana and Papaw Welch were called to tell them, instead of coming to the drugstore, to just meet us in Parkersburg because we could wait no longer.

By this time many prayer warriors had been contacted and prayers were going up from all over. Elder Baron Claypool and Sister Jenni Claypool later said that when they got the news, they were in a grocery store in Ohio, and they went straight to their knees to pray. Prayer chains were being formed and folks close to Zach were seeking God for a miracle.

About 10 minutes later, about 3:15 PM, I called Brad back, knowing it had been about a half an hour. I kind of knew that by the end of this phone call, I would know the fate of my youngest son, because it had been so long.

Brad stated that the ambulance had arrived and they were initially working on him on the field, but by then they had him inside the ambulance. Brad thought he had overheard one of the EMTs ask if they should "call it" (referring to officially declaring the time of death at the moment of ceasing efforts to resuscitate).

Brad said that the ambulance was rocking back and forth. The saints waiting outside continued to pray, laying hands on the sides of the ambulance in travail before God and speaking the name of Jesus in faith mixed with desperation.

Within a minute of being on the phone with Brad, the ambulance stopped rocking.

The saints that were praying were anxious as to why it stopped moving. Had the emergency medical technicians given up the resuscitation efforts?

The doors opened up, and an EMT stepped out with his head down. Time stood still for those around the ambulance.

The EMT looked up and said, "We got him back." He said, "We have a pulse and we are taking him to Camden Clark Hospital in Parkersburg [West Virginia]."

There is no doubt in our minds that angels were dispatched to that field in Parkersburg, West Virginia,

to start the heart of Zachary Patrick Sandy. *No doubt! Hallelujah! God stepped onto the scene!*

One of the EMTs later stated that it was the strongest pulse he had ever gotten on a resuscitation patient in all of his years on the squad.

Chapter 7:
Valley of the Shadow of Death

"Yea, though I walk through the valley of the shadow of death, I will fear no evil: for thou art with me" (Psalm 23:4).

he trip to Camden Clark Hospital in Parkersburg was an interesting one. By the time we reached Doddridge County, one of the EMTs in the ambulance called my phone. He reassured me that they were going to do everything they could for my son. Zach was fairly stable, but in critical condition. They were not sure the extent of his injuries, but the burns that they could see did not seem serious. He did explain that when lightning strikes, what is happening on the inside, hidden from view, is mostly where the danger is. Lightning can superheat the bones or bone marrow to a temperature of around 200 degrees and cook organs, muscle, etc., from the inside out.

The EMT said, "It could be a couple of days before we know the extent of the damage."

After hanging up with him, we continued to call folks, and we fielded numerous calls. We continually shared the phone charger, and at a few points lost service completely.

Somewhere near Ritchie County, John sighed and said, "We are not going to have enough fuel to get there." So we planned to stop near Ritchie County High School for fuel. Somewhere along Route 50, something caught my eye in the back window of John's car. Elder Keith Fought and Sister Lisa Fought were following close behind us. (We later learned that Pastor Doug Joseph and Sister LaDonna Joseph had finally received our voice mail messages via cell phone, while they were on their way home from a meeting in Charleston, and they were fervently praying while desperately trying to get to the hospital as well.)

We stopped for gas, and while John pumped fuel, Cheri went to the restroom.

Upon returning to our car, a WV State Trooper had begun to fill his cruiser with fuel close to John's vehicle. He saw us scurrying around and asked if everything was OK. The trooper indicated that if there was anything wrong, he could assist us. Cheri told him that our son had been in an accident in Parkersburg and we were in a hurry. He told us to be safe.

We hurried back to the car and jumped back onto Route 50 to continue to Parkersburg, with the Fought's close behind us.

John joked, "I hope that trooper stays there a few more minutes until I get out of sight."

The ride was an event in itself. John tried his best to get us to Parkersburg as quickly as he could. John and Zach were pretty tight; they went fishing together and toured the mall from time to time. I knew that he was reacting to this as if it was one of his own kids.

A few times I asked John to slow down a bit. At one point, while going around a curve in the road, I promise you the car was on only two wheels! Thank God for keeping his hand on us. (And thank you, John, for getting us to Parkersburg so quickly.)

When we entered into town the traffic was bad. Of course, when you are in a hurry, any traffic seems bad. It felt like it took forever to get across town. When we approached Camden Clark Hospital, Paul Glaspell Jr. (Brad's father) was in the parking lot motioning where to park. John maneuvered around and parked.

We jumped out of the car and ran toward the emergency room, while being greeted by Paul Glaspell

Jr., Jesse Glaspell, Brad Glaspell, Ralph Tisdale, Caleb Tisdale, Brother Nelson, and Jim Workman.

The hospital's chaplain met Cheri at the door, wanting her to fill out paperwork. While we had been in transit, the hospital had been frantically trying to get information about Zach. Because he was not an officially registered camper, the camp staff did not know anything about Zach—barely even his age, let alone any medical history.

Cheri pushed past the chaplain, saying she was going to see her son. All of the folks there from the campground greeted us as we rushed by.

We were finally able to see Zach. He looked like he was sleeping peacefully. The doctors were there immediately, explaining what the purpose was for each tube and wire. Cheri and John and I began talking to Zach, telling him that we were there with him.

Cheri repeatedly told Zach, "Mommy is here now, and you are going to be OK."

The three of us spoke a short-but-earnest prayer over Zach. John tried to take a picture of Zach with his phone, but he was quickly scolded by one of the doctors.

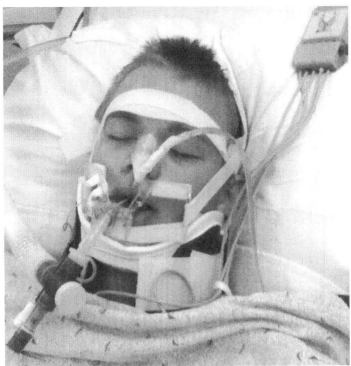

Zach was under such heavy sedation that it intentionally suppresses one's natural instinct to breathe (this was so the machine could breathe for him). Despite this, at times, Zach would try to breathe over top of the machine.

"Do not do that again," the doctor said.

We have no idea why he said that.

One of Zach's socks was on the floor under the bed that was holding Zach.

As I approached Zach's room, the first thing I noticed was his urine bag under the bed. It was bright red due to blood in the urine. I mentioned to Cheri that it was a sign of major internal damage.

The doctors informed us that there was absolutely no way of telling what was going on inside of Zach's body—neither physically nor neurologically. They indicated that organs could be fried, and the lungs would probably be nonfunctional.

The doctors said that they had no way of knowing how to treat Zach; one reason they gave for this is practically no one ever survives a direct strike.

They had already planned to send Zach to Ruby Memorial Hospital in Morgantown. Even then EMTs were working to prep Zach for the trip.

I stayed with Zach, while Cheri went out to find the chaplain. She filled out the paperwork, and she was introduced to the Tisdales. She spoke with everyone in the waiting room. Pastor Ralph Tisdale later recalled something Cheri said as he spoke with her.

Cheri had told him, "This will be for the glory of God."

Cheri had no inside information to make such a statement. She saw what everyone else saw—her son's half lifeless body in an emergency room. Yet she spoke faith that day; she knew that her God could do anything, and that her God is the Miracle Worker.

The doctors came in and confirmed that Zach would be transported by ambulance to Morgantown as soon as they secured a team. I inquired about riding in the ambulance, because I had just ridden one hour to get to my son and I was not going to leave his side.

The driver tried to burst my bubble, saying that I could not ride along due to company policy.

I replied, "Call your supervisor, rewrite the policy, whatever—I am going with my son if I have to tie myself to the bumper."

Eventually it was agreed that I could ride in the front of the ambulance. The driver told me that we were going to be running with lights on and using the siren when needed. Zach was considered a "Level One" trauma. Phone calls were made to all those on their way to Parkersburg, instructing them to turn around and go to Morgantown.

It took a few more minutes than expected to get going from the hospital. Cheri rode with John back across Route 50 to Morgantown, about a 95-minute drive. Finally we left Parkersburg for Morgantown.

I made several phone calls to a lot of folks, checking with my wife and Rusty every now and then. I got a call from Ashley and Linda Vaughn in Georgia, saying that they had gotten to my Mom before she saw it on Facebook. Mom talked to me on the phone. Her voice quivered some, but the Vaughn's had done an awesome job of comforting her. Linda had read several scriptural passages to her, as well as an inspirational poem that encouraged faith. When she read the poetic piece, she replaced the word "you" with Zach's name. It was very powerful and touching. The following were included among the faith-building passages of scripture that she read to Zach's Mamaw:

"As soon as Jesus heard the word that was spoken, he saith unto the ruler of the synagogue, Be not afraid, only believe" (Mark 5:36).

"I shall not die, but live, and declare the works of the LORD" (Psalms 118:17).

"Behold, the eye of the LORD is upon them that fear him, upon them that hope in his mercy; To deliver their soul from death, and to keep them alive in famine. Our soul waiteth for the LORD: he is our help and our shield. For our heart shall rejoice in him, because we have trusted in his holy name. Let thy mercy, O LORD, be upon us, according as we hope in thee" (Psalms 33:18-22).

Student-campers at VA District UPCI youth camp praying for Zach.

Prayer Support from Everywhere

We later learned that the Virginia District UPCI youth camp had heard of the accident. Brandon Sandy, Samuel Vaughn, Madeline Vaughn, and Morgan Hurley were there, among others who would have attended West Virginia youth camp with Zach. All the youth were gathered into the sanctuary for immediate prayer.

By that time there were hundreds, if not thousands, of folks praying for a miracle. Eventually confirmations of prayer came in from many US states, some Canadian provinces, and several places overseas including Brazil and Africa.

Back in the ambulance I was quickly losing battery strength on my phone. Without it I would be unable to communicate with anyone. I asked the driver what kind of charger he had for his phone. He reached on the dash and grabbed a charger that exactly matched the one for my phone. *Thank you, Jesus!*

As we traveled, it was another time when I had a few minutes to commune with God.

I talked with Him, man to Miracle Worker; man to Jehovah-Shalom (the LORD our Peace); man to Jehovah-Jireh (the LORD our Provider); man to Jehovah-Rapha (the LORD our Healer); man to El Shaddai (God Almighty); man to "The Great I AM."

Two or three times the driver said, "Excuse me?"

I had to tell him that I was not talking to him, I was praying.

Somewhere along Route 50, something happened in the back of the ambulance that caused a huge crashing sound. I panicked and turned to see what was going on. The driver explained that something had fallen over; no problem. I looked back several times to see them just monitoring Zach.

"Fear thou not; for I am with thee: be not dismayed; for I am thy God: I will strengthen thee; yea, I will help thee; yea, I will uphold thee with the right hand of my righteousness" (Isaiah 41:10).

Several times Rusty sent me text messages wondering where we were. While we were at the interchange of Route 50 and Interstate 79, as we passed through the traffic light and onto the on-ramp to I-79, I looked and saw Sister Cindy Murphy waiting for the light to change. She saw me at the last moment and waved.

I learned that a crowd was gathering at Ruby Memorial's emergency room waiting area. Somewhere between 50 to 70 folks had already gathered.

When we arrived I saw Rusty and his Papaw Welch standing outside, and through the windows I could see several folks anxious for Zach's arrival.

The ambulance stopped a few feet past the entrance, and I got out. Rusty instantly grabbed me. It was an intense hug. No doubt the horror of what happened to his little brother, and the anticipation of finally getting to see him, was overwhelming to say the least. Cheri joined the hug and we tried to strengthen and encourage each other. Pastor and Sister Joseph and many others met us there, all speaking words of faith to us.

The EMTs unloaded Zach and took him into the emergency room. Most folks got to see him on all the equipment as he was carried past them. Rusty has testified that he knew he had to say something to his brother as he was passing by. He decided to say something that Zach would have said to him.

Rusty said, "Be strong, Zach!"

They wheeled Zach into the emergency room. It wasn't long before the staff came to meet with Cheri, Rusty, and me. They informed us that Zach would immediately be flown to West Penn Burn Center in Pittsburgh, PA. The doctor mentioned that Ruby had tried to defer Zach straight to Pittsburgh, but they could not secure a chopper until he arrived there.

Cheri, Rusty and I got to go see Zach; they were prepping him for the helicopter flight. Cheri went to get her Mom and Dad, because the hospital staff said that only immediate family could see him. My faith was strong, but I was worried about the urine bag having appeared blood red in the Parkersburg Hospital. But as I looked at it in that moment, the urine was very brown in color.

I asked the nurse, "That being brown is better than it being red, right?"

She replied, "No you would want it to be red, really."

(In retrospect, that detail really weighed on my mind a lot during the trip that we undertook soon after to Pennsylvania.)

There in Morgantown, the emergency room waiting area was completely packed with folks waiting to see Zach. As soon as I knew that we were going to travel again, I went to the waiting area to greet friends and family. A lot of folks had come to our rescue and to support us in time of need.

I asked our pastor, Brother Doug Joseph, to gather everyone together for prayer outside in the parking area. A massive crowd gathered in a broad circle near the entrance of the emergency room.

Pastor Joseph spoke a few words of faith and hope. Soon we began to pray. It was a powerful, public prayer service as many Spirit-filled believers entered into fervent intercession for Zach.

After the prayer I remarked, "I would not be surprised if Zach got up off of that bed and walked out of the emergency room right now!"

The hospital staff really wanted to get Zach on his way to Pittsburgh in a hurry. That doctor reiterated to us that lightning has the potential to heat the inside of the body, bones, or bone marrow to 180 degrees and basically cook the strike victim from the inside out. They were not sure what was going on inside of Zach.

Just as we concluded praying, a HealthNet helicopter lifted off from the rooftop. We surmised that it was most likely Zach.

We knew the trip to Pittsburgh would be a long one. Because of how much faster the helicopter could fly, Zach would beat us to Pittsburgh by about two hours. It was agreed that Cheri and I were going to drive her parent's car, while John & Tracy and Rusty & Hannah followed us in their cars.

We all stopped at McDonald's on the way out. We weren't sure when we would be able to eat again. We went in to eat and tried to gather ourselves and come to grips with what had just happened. We all charged our phones as we ate. There was no way of knowing how Zach was doing or whether he had arrived. We finished eating, and we decided that John would take the lead, since he knows Pittsburgh.

We made some phone calls to get the address to put into the GPS. We called a hospital in Pittsburgh, but it ended up being the wrong hospital. However, the lady who answered was very nice and gave us the phone number for the West Penn Hospital.

Pittsburgh has always been a tough place to navigate. Seeking a certain destination can be confusing. Trying to find our way there actually took our minds off of Zach a little. Once we reached the sprawling hospital complex, parked in the parking garage, and found the actual Burn Center within the hospital, we tried to find the nurse's station.

Two doctors and a nurse immediately came out to talk to us. They told us that Zach was stable, and that they were getting him set up in his room. It would be a few minutes before we could see him.

At times on the way up, I had discussed the urine bag with Cheri. We were still very concerned about the urine bag having been red and then brown. We were terrified that something bad was going on inside of Zach's body, but we continued to pray within ourselves about the urine color.

We began to look around for the waiting room. I turned to walk away, but then I stopped. I wondered if the nurse would tell me about the urine bag.

So I said, "Excuse me—"

The nurse turned back toward us.

I asked her, "This may sound weird, but could you take a peek at Zach's urine bag for us?"

She had a look of surprise, but said she would take a look and be right back. The nurse disappeared behind the automatic doors, and it seemed like forever before she came back. She came through the doors with her head tilted sideways, and a puzzled look on her face. Then she spoke a miracle to us.

She stated, "I'm not sure what the concern was, but the urine in the bag is clear."

Hallelujah!

"Yea, though I walk through the valley of the shadow of death, I will fear no evil: for thou art with me" (Psalm 23:4).

Our pastor and his wife, Doug and LaDonna Joseph, with us at West Penn Burn Center in Pittsburgh, PA.

Chapter 8:
In the Land of a
Thousand Questions

ohn and Tracy had found the waiting room, along with Rusty and Hannah, and we joined them. Faith and hope hovered in that waiting room, surely due to the Lord honoring all the prayers. Never was a negative word to be spoken in that room in all the following seven days while we were there. Well, doctors would speak of doubt and no hope, but family and friends only spoke of hope and faith.

We again plugged in all our phones, and we sat down to unwind from our trip. A nurse came to the door of the waiting room and asked for Zach's parents. We went back to see Zach.

On the way the nurse asked, "Are all those people back there in the waiting area part of Zach's family?"

We said, "Yes."

She said, "I will go get them, and let them come and see him also."

Zach looked like he was just asleep. He looked good for someone who had been struck by lightning just seven hours before. The nurse began to tell us about what they were going to do that night for Zach. Then she explained that the next morning they were going to do tests to make sure his neck wasn't broken, and then they would see about removing the breathing machine and tube later in the afternoon, to see if he could breathe on his own.

Finally she said, "You all need to get some rest."

We told her, "We aren't going far. We are just going to the waiting room."

We all went to waiting room and put blankets on the floor for sleeping that night.

The nurse walked in to check on us sometime later, and she said, "Oh no, I can't have you all sleeping on this floor. If someone will help me I will get all of you recliners to sleep in tonight, but we have to return them first thing in the morning."

Cheri and I got a few short naps during the night. It was a continual up and down, as they let us into the hospital room any time we wanted to go. Rusty woke up at one point in the night and searched for me. He found me in Zach's room with my head resting on the bed next to Zach.

Rusty asked, "If we play music from the iPod, do you think Zach would hear it?"

We agreed that it was worth a try. Rusty flipped through the songs, deciding which one to play.

A second later he said, "This is Zach's favorite."

A song by Planetshakers entitled "Nothing is Impossible" began to play.

The chorus says, "Through You I can do anything. I can do all things, 'cause it is You that gives me strength. *Nothing is impossible!*"

The verse of the song says, "I'm not going to live by what I see. I'm not going to live by what I feel."

What we saw was Zach laying there with a machine breathing for him, and our Zach could not talk to us.

The song also says, "Deep down I know that You're here with me, and I know that You can do anything!"

Deep down we believed that God was able to perform a miracle in this situation.

The song also repeats several times "I Believe! I Believe!"

Cheri went to check on Zach at one point, to find John sitting by the doors that enter the burn unit; he had been pacing the floor a lot. Since he had worked Tuesday night from 11:00 PM to 7:00 AM, and had gotten only an hour or so of sleep before we woke him up with the news, he was going on 30-plus hours since he had really slept.

They went back to check on Zach. It looked like Zach was trying to open his eyes to look around, so Cheri came out to get me. Zach was not able to see, but it was exciting to think maybe he could! We were looking for any sign.

All night long, at different times each one of us was up, pacing the floor and praying. Morning came, and Cheri and I vowed not to leave his bedside until Zach was OK. We stuck close to the doctors and nurses, waiting for some kind of good news.

John went for coffee and came back with some honeybuns and coffee. I did not eat. I knew that with my diabetes my blood sugar was probably raging because of all of the stress. I knew I had to eat, but I was just not in the mood.

At 10:27 AM I received a text on my phone from Regina Mealey, a coworker of mine at United Hospital Center (UHC). She indicated that she and about 20 of our coworkers had gone to the chapel at the hospital and lit a candle, prayed for Zach, and conversed some. The hospital chaplain had joined them. I can't remember much more about Thursday before 4:00 PM.

We were constantly watching the nurses' station for anything about Zach and what they were going to do. I remember that at one point a group of doctors came in, and there were surgeons with them. I was worried they might want to do an exploratory surgery to see what damage, if any, was done to his organs. I guess I watch too much "Life and Trauma in the ER" (a cable show on the Lifetime channel).

Visitors came, and many phone calls came in. Cell phones were being charged everywhere. All of us were constantly on the phone with folks that encouraged us and spoke words of faith to us. I thank God that He has put wonderful people in our lives over the years that pray for us, love us for who we are, and are not afraid to speak words of faith to us.

John mentioned several times that you could feel the prayers of people everywhere filling the hallways of the West Penn Hospital. As horrified as we were just one day earlier, the power of prayer and a comforting peace that only God can give, came over us and settled in the waiting area, the hallways, and Zach's room. We all were so overwhelmed by the many text messages and Facebook messages that said, "We are praying for you." I personally do not need any big-shot televangelist praying for me any more than someone I do not even know getting word to me that they are praying for my son.

At one point we were explaining to the nightshift nurse what had happened to Zach. The departing staff had briefed her. We told her that Zach was without a pulse, and that within seconds of the folks praying with their hands on the ambulance, the EMTs got a pulse.

The nurse shivered and rubbed her arms and said, "Wow! That gives me goose bumps."

I will quote from a sermon preached by Pastor Jeff Arnold of Gainesville, Florida: "Those aren't goose bumps," he said, "that is the Holy Ghost!"

I knew then that Cheri was absolutely correct in what she had stated in the emergency room in Parkersburg, after she saw Zach for the first time following the lightning strike: "This will be for the glory of God!"

As we watched Zach sleep under heavy sedation with machines breathing for him, different ones from the family mentioned moments of Zach's life and how he had impacted them. The flood of memories ranged from a funny moment here and there to the struggles he had when he was born.

Not knowing what was going on inside of Zach's body was like a minefield of the mind for us. The doctors could not tell us for sure what would become of Zach. We sought to dodge the mines of doubt and despair, but some nagging questions were unavoidable: Will he wake up? If he does will he know us? Will he not be paralyzed? Will he ever be able to function properly?

At that point, if not allowing for a miracle or a series of miracles, the realistic answer to all those questions was resoundingly in the negative!

Sometime later, during February 2013 at a UPCI youth conference in Charleston, WV, Brother Lee Stoneking, a great man of God, approached us. He did not know fully what had happened to Zach except that he had been struck by lightning.

Brother Stoneking came to pray for Zach, and he looked at Cheri and me and said, "This young man's brain should have been mincemeat." He continued, "Do not take for granted what was, when he lay in that hospital bed."

That confirmed to me that God had continued to do miracle after miracle, even after He had resurrected Zach.

It was surely due to prayers from everyone everywhere. I took several walks and prayed to God. I can remember seeing just about every family member take a moment to lay their hand on Zach or lay their head on Zach's bed and pray. At one point I went out and came back to find Cheri alone with Zach. She had ahold of his hand and had laid her head on Zach's stomach and was crying and praying. I stepped back out of the room and let her pray. As I have heard many times in the past year or so, thank God for praying mothers.

We logged into Facebook.com as often as we could. Messages kept pouring in. Lots of folks said later that Facebook was how they followed Zach's progress. Zach actually had 1,800 friends added to his Facebook. Cheri and I kept his Facebook account going until Zach was able to. Many calls came to the phone in the waiting room.

My brother, John, was voted in as "The Public Relations Guy" for this event. Every time a call came in from a TV station or anyone we did not know, we would defer the call to our PR guy. Also, Pastor Doug Joseph was dubbed the photographer/video producer for this miracle. Over 10,000 folks have seen his videos about Zach on YouTube.com and in many church services.

Chapter 9:
The Great Awakening

"Wherefore he saith, Awake thou that sleepest, and arise from the dead, and Christ shall give thee light" (Ephesians 5:14).

bout noon, the nursing staff came to us and said that there was a possibility that in a few hours they were going to try to remove the breathing tube and disconnect the breathing machine. They were waiting for some test results to come back first. A major concern was that once a breathing machine is removed, it is problematic to have to reinsert it if it was really still needed after all.

At about 3:30 PM a large group of medical staff came to Zach's room. They said that we would have to go to the waiting area while while they unhooked everything and removed the breathing machine.

I asked one of the doctors if I would be permitted back in the room before Zach woke up. Zach has always told Cheri and me that his biggest fear is waking up in a hospital with wires and tubes all over him and having no knowledge of what happened. I knew I just had to be there when his eyes opened. The doctor assured me that we would be allowed back in before Zach awoke.

He said, "It will take him a while to come out from under sedation."

Cheri, Rusty, and I went back at first. Zach was moving his legs a little. The three of us talked in Zach's ear and Cheri sang to him.

One particular nurse said over and over, "We need him to talk."

I thought to myself, *Well wouldn't that be fantastic?*

That nurse became so overbearing that Cheri left the room and sent her Mom back. Rusty went out with his Mom to calm her down. Most everyone else from the waiting room were then just outside the double doors that led to the burn unit, waiting for good news.

Approximately 20 minutes later, Zach seemed to open his eyes a few times. Nana continued to talk to Zach and sing in his ear. A few minutes later, Zach opened his eyes and looked at me. I saw his mouth move a little. I instantly put my ear to his mouth, not knowing what to expect. For as long as I have breath, I will always thank God for what happened next.

In a faint, scratchy voice Zach said, "Hungry," and closed his eyes again.

Overall this experience had been one that I hope no one else ever has to go through, but we were overjoyed when Zach regained a pulse on the softball field in Parkersburg almost exactly one day earlier. We again rejoiced when the urine bag cleared up in just six or seven hours. Nevertheless, I will declare that at that point I was ready to take "a timeout for a shout!" as Pastor Joseph would put it (a joyful declaration inspired by Pastor Ron Libby of Gaithersburg, MD).

Nana continued to talk to Zach, asking him over and over what he wanted to eat. Zach opened his eyes a few minutes later and focused on his Nana.

She repeated the question, "What do you want to eat? I will go get it."

I saw Zach's mouth moving again. I leaned down to hear.

Zach said, "Hamburger."

Nana Welch hurried to get Cheri and Rusty. My tears started to flow. I gave a fist pump in the air.

I said, "Yeeeeeeessssssss!" as I was thanking God over and over.

Zach was going to be OK!

"And all things, whatsoever ye shall ask in prayer, believing, ye shall receive" (Matthew 21:22).

We knew that Zach is always hungry, and he loves hamburgers. Cheri and Rusty came in the room, both moved to tears by the news. Rusty put his arm around me and repeated what he told me the first time I got to talk to him after the accident.

Rusty said, "Z is going to be OK."

Cheri and Rusty often referred to Zach as "Z." A few more minutes passed before Zach opened his eyes again. He looked at his Mom and then looked at Rusty. Both were crying.

Zach then looked at me and said, "Why are Mommy and Bubby crying?"

I wasn't sure what to say besides, "They are happy that you are going to be OK."

Zach then reached up, took my hand, pulled it tight to his chest, and said, "We need to pray."

At that moment Pastor Doug Joseph snapped an iconic photo that became the trademark of a miracle among the prayer movement that had sprouted up on account of Zach.

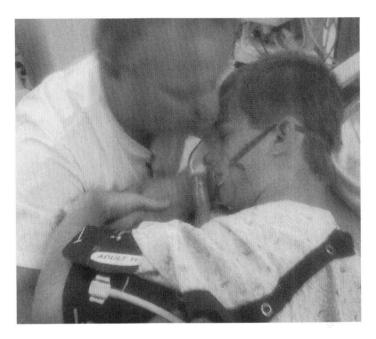

Just like many, many times before, when the boys were young and on through their teenage years, there we were, Cheri, Rusty, Zach and I, praying together again. It was a short prayer. Zach fell off to sleep again.

Later Zach bumped Rusty's arm and asked his brother to get him a Gatorade. After we checked with the nursing staff to be sure it would be permitted, Rusty immediately went downstairs and got Z a Gatorade.

We tried to ensure that everyone who was waiting was permitted to go back to see Zach, preferably while he was awake. Many came to Zach's room and prayed with him. For the most part, the hospital let us do whatever we needed to as far as letting folks visit.

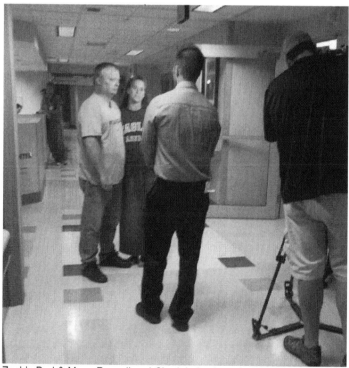

Zach's Dad & Mom, Russell and Cheri, being interviewed by Channel 4, WTAE—first of many media crews that would eventually cover the story.

Both the newspaper and WTAP TV from Parkersburg, WV, kept in touch and reported often on Zach's progress. WTAE TV channel 4 from there in Pittsburgh asked permission to interview Cheri and me. We talked it over with family. We sort of wondered why a Pittsburgh TV station would want to do a story on a boy from West Virginia. We all agreed that since the news was usually always full of violence and other bad things, a story with a happy ending would be a welcome change.

We were beginning to understand the widespread impact that this miracle was going to have, as well as how many folks it would reach.

We agreed to the interview, although we did not grant permission to interview Zach, who was still fuzzy. We just didn't feel he was ready. We didn't want Zach to be embarrassed later.

The interview went fine. Everyone in the waiting room gathered around to watch the news at 6:00 PM, just to see how the reporters portrayed it.

WTAE news ended their report by saying, "It has been an emotional roller coaster for the family, waiting for good news. They say they got that good news, and they are calling this *a miracle!*"

Eventually KDKA channel 2 from Pittsburgh came to do an interview. They also inquired about interviewing Zach, and again we explained that it was just not time yet. In days that followed, WCHS TV (Charleston, WV), WBOY TV channel 12 (Clarksburg, WV), and the Exponent-Telegram newspaper (Clarksburg, WV) also interviewed either Cheri or me and ran reports. They all closely followed Zach's progress.

Chapter 10:
The Long Way Home
(AKA Miracle Road)

Zach progressively got better. At first he wanted to sleep all the time, but that was OK. We allowed him to rest. He could not walk. He scooted into a wheelchair to visit the waiting room for a few minutes at a time, then for longer periods as more time passed.

Zach had to be helped to the restroom. He tried to get out of bed and tried to stand up out of the wheelchair several times. We had to tell him that he could not get up yet. When he tried, his legs just wouldn't do it. His knees would buckle. After two days, Zach began physical therapy. He worked two hours per day on strengthening his leg muscles. As the sedative wore off for good, you could see Zach getting frustrated. He never complained or questioned whether all this was permanent or not. He was just aggravated that he could not get up and go.

On Thursday night John and Tracy had planned to get Cheri and me out of the hospital for the night. They insisted that we go with them to a local hotel to spend the night. My other brother, David Sandy, his wife, Brenda, and their son, Brandon, along with Ashley and Linda Vaughn and their family, stayed at the hospital.

Cheri and I looked at each other, and we both thought, *No way we are leaving.*

However, as they insisted that we go, and we knew God was looking over Zach, we agreed to go. Thanks again to everyone that helped us.

We traveled a short while to the hotel and got in the room. We were all mentally and physically exhausted. Actually, we were way past exhausted. We talked for a bit about the past few days' events, and then we lay down to sleep. Sleep? I think we slept a few times, for a few minutes. I woke up and was ready to walk back and check on Zach, only to realize we were not at the hospital. A couple of times I wanted to ask John to take me back over to the hospital to see if everything was OK. I think I did call Ashley one time during the night.

At one point during the night I did catch my wife snoozing. I began thanking God that he allowed her to rest her mind, even if only for just a few minutes. As a husband and father, I have always tried to go out of my way to protect my family. I knew this tragedy was not my fault, yet I wished I could take away the fear and horror of the past two days and make it all better for my wife, Rusty, and all of the family for that matter. Nevertheless, I knew that God was taking care of it. I just knew it.

"Be strong and of a good courage, fear not, nor be afraid of them: for the Lord thy God, he it is that doth go with thee; he will not fail thee, nor forsake thee" (Deuteronomy 31:6).

Sometime around 5:00 AM I must have dozed off, because I had a nasty nightmare and was trying to wake up.

Cheri, John, and Tracy later told me that I was screaming "No, Brad! No, Brad! Please, no!" Brad was my cousin who had called me that day to inform me that Zach had been struck by lightning.

They got me awake and John promised to take me immediately to the hospital to check on Zach. Zach was in good hands with his aunts and uncles.

The waiting area was full of family and friends. The cell phones couldn't stay charged long enough. The phone in the waiting room stayed busy. The iPods couldn't respond to Facebook messages quickly enough. There were so many devices being charged that I am not sure how the other areas of the hospital were getting any electricity.

Pillows and blankets were everywhere. All day long, someone was catching a nap in the recliners. Zach's cousins were playing games around the table. Drinks were getting spilled in the carpet. Everyone took turns going to the cafeteria to eat. Folks brought food to us. The table was full of food constantly.

The housekeeper came to the door of the waiting room one day. I saw her look in and shake her head and turn and walk away. I went to the door and stopped her. I told her that I would empty the garbage when it was full; otherwise we were going to be there for a while.

After the first few days the doctors spoke to us less and less. One day the medical staff proclaimed that they were going to have a meeting with all personnel at 10:00 AM concerning Zach. We waited and waited to hear something from it. Finally at 3:00 PM we insisted to know what they came up with. They didn't really tell us much of what the meeting was about.

Deanna, one of Zach's nurses, was especially helpful; she is the one that got us the recliners the first night. She just loved Zach, and Zach soaked it all up. When you are in the hospital, it helps a ton if the staff is pleasant. We were stressed enough wondering if our son was going to be OK. God sent a helpful, pleasant nursing staff to comfort us.

Zach was struggling to stand and walk. Getting to the bathroom was a chore for him. His knee was giving out on him, and he simply had no strength whatsoever in his legs. To get him to the restroom, one had to take him as far as they could, then stand behind him and hold him until he finished, then help him back to his wheelchair. Zach was lunging out of the bed and wheelchair, trying to stand up. (Earlier, while first coming around, he had pulled out four IV-feed lines and had pulled his catheter out twice. **Ouch!**) He was not combative; he simply was not yet off the medicine that had kept him sedated.

The speech therapist worked with Zach a lot. She asked him a lot of questions.

At one point early on, she asked him, "What color is a banana?" Surprisingly, Zach could not answer the question.

The accident happened on Wednesday, July 11, 2012. On Friday, July 13, Zach was given a memory and competency test. He scored three points out of 30 possible points. The following Monday, July 16, Zach took the same test again, and he scored 27 out of 30. God was doing miracles every day.

Needless to say, Zach recovered his ability to recall that a banana is yellow. Eventually he grew frustrated by them repeatedly asking him what color a banana is. To this day I will ask him the same question if I want to kid around with him.

The hospital was very accommodating. Different folks sat with Zach each night, as Cheri and I went to hotel late at night and rested. Family, friends and our church helped with the hotel cost. I cannot say enough: we were overwhelmed with the compassion and love that was shown to Zach and Cheri and I.

A sweet lady named Joy Watkins talked with Zach a lot, and one afternoon she helped us take Zach outside in his wheelchair, to a park beside the hospital. We circled the park a few times. We decided that it was too hot out, and we returned to the room.

Above: Family and friends praying for Zach while he was out in the waiting area for a visit. Between a lot of sleeping and some therapy, he spent as much time as he could visiting with folks in the waiting area.

Zach did physical therapy a few hours each day. He slept the rest of the time, unless he had company. He started spending time in the waiting area to make it easier for folks to see him.

Several folks came to see Zach, including Kim & Katie McCloud, the Thomas family, the Bayles family, the Channel family (shown above, entering), etc. Many of our Christian Apostolic Church family came. Most of Cheri's and my family were there.

The hospital began to talk about sending Zach to a rehab center. This news caused some confusion for friends and family who wanted to travel in and visit; they weren't sure if or when he was being transferred, so only a few folks came to see Zach during that period. This affected the last few days there.

The doctors pointed out that Zach's muscle enzyme levels were grossly high. They directed for fluids to be forced into him to level off those enzymes. In the day or so following that directive, Zach actually drank so much that his potassium and other levels bottomed out. They had to change his diet and give him vitamins. The enzymes leveled off and the doctors spoke of releasing him. Zach was all in favor of that.

It had been mentioned that in lightning strike victims, their burns almost always get worse over time instead of better (because of internal damage coming to the surface over time). In Zach's case, we saw the opposite. His Uncle John had commented that on the day of the strike, as Zach was moved from hospital to hospital, each time we got to see Zach his burns looked better instead of worse!

Only five days after he suffered a lightning strike to the head—in which somewhere between 20,000 to 60,000 volts of electricity had raged through his body—the burn center doctors of West Penn Hospital were in agreement that Zach Sandy was no longer a burn patient. Zach was now a rehab patient.

Two days later, Zach was released from West Penn Burn Center in Pittsburgh, PA, and transferred to

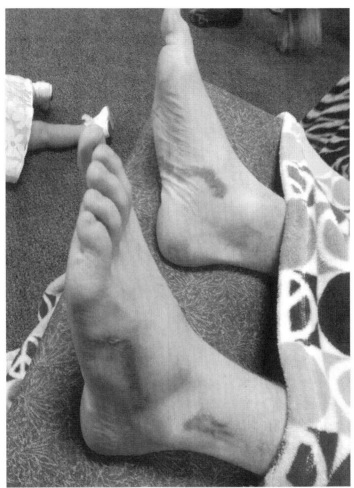

Zach's feet as they appeared on July 15, 2012, about four and a half days after the lightning strike. These burns and markings were evidence of where the lightning exited his body, resulting in multiple holes punched in both his socks and shoes. This photo was taken while Zach was in the waiting room visiting with friends and family.

HealthSouth Mountain View Regional Rehabilitation Hospital in Morgantown, WV. This occurred on Wednesday, July 18, in the afternoon—exactly one week removed from when Zach endured tens of thousands of volts of electricity charging through him from the top of his head to the soles of his feet. Amazing!

We all shouted, "Hallelujah!"

HealthSouth Mountain View Regional Rehabilitation Hospital, Morgantown, WV

Zach was transported by an ambulance service that was based out of Pittsburgh. He was carried from West Penn to HealthSouth, which is located much closer to our home than where we were previously in Pittsburgh. This new location was only about 35 minutes' driving time from our house.

Upon our arrival at the rehab center, Zach and I were greeted by the medical staff, which included a young lady who knew Zach from church camp. Felicia Parker had tears flowing from her eyes as she welcomed us. She helped Zach get settled in.

Zach was assigned to a room in which a previous occupant had been regarded as a "walking miracle." Because of this, a sign (shown above) on the wall identified the hallway leading to that room as "Miracle Road." How fitting!

Zach's appetite was not very good when he arrived at HealthSouth. At specific times throughout the day he would attend therapy sessions. Some were for strength, while others were for balance. He also spent time in the pool, doing exercises.

For the first few days, if Zach was not at his therapy sessions, it was because he was in bed resting due to pain in his hips and legs. Some may think that no true miracles were done unless there was nothing at all left for Zach to fight through personally, but that simply is not accurate. Regardless of any battles left for Zach to face, we know that various amazing miracles were provided along the way.

By that point we had received thousands of messages from people praying and seeking God for a full recovery for Zach. He had already come so far, but he still had a long way to go.

Zach was not eating much, hardly anything at all. We sought foods that would get him to eat. Some folks (I cannot remember exactly who all) went to get foods for him from various places: Buffalo Wild Wings, Kegler's, Applebee's, and Chick-Fil-A, etc. Once Chick-Fil-A actually called us for our order and had food sent to us!

The John Sandy family with Zach the day he arrived at HealthSouth.

To greet and fellowship with his visitors, eventually Zach made trips to a courtyard outside, or to the main lobby inside, and sometimes to an extra room made available by the staff at HealthSouth. Many people visited from all over; family, acquaintances, student friends from high school, friends from several churches.

Among the many visitors were members of the West Virginia University football and basketball teams. Because of Zach's love of sports and his history of athleticism, this was a real treat. Even more important was the role these events played in serving as a witness to the team members of God's existence and power.

The team members brought Zach gifts that he was so pleased to receive.

As nice as the athlete visits were, something even better was in store for Zach that day.

On July 19 Zach got to meet Caleb Tisdale, the first to respond with CPR.

On Thursday, July 19, 2012, Zach got to meet face to face with Caleb Tisdale and Caleb's wife, Bailey. Caleb was the young minister whom Zach had met five minutes prior to starting the softball game at camp. Caleb had performed "Holy Ghost CPR" on Zach back on July 11. Caleb had given breaths to Zach, and then while doing chest compressions, Caleb would pray to God in tongues.

The visit was much anticipated, as Caleb also met the family. Russell and Cheri and the family were so overwhelmed that they had no adequate words to express how grateful they were for Caleb's quick actions, knowledge of CPR, and—perhaps most of all—his perseverance and never-give-up approach. Heartfelt thanks, hugs, and a whole lot of tears didn't seem like enough. Caleb seemed to downplay his role in the whole process. Sure, most anyone would try to help in an emergency and do whatever they could to help, but we are convinced that Caleb and the staff at Spreading Truth Ministries were anointed in the way they responded that day. The Sandy and Tisdale families, and Spreading Truth Ministries, are forever linked and now sealed as family.

Although Zach was in pain and his legs were very restless, he was getting comfortable in his new surroundings at HealthSouth. He was teasing the nursing staff and making new friends. As time progressed he got around the facility more and more.

That second day with Zach at HealthSouth, Cheri, Rusty, and I took off while Zach was in therapy. We traveled to the nearest church that we knew, which was Riverside Ministries (UPCI), in Morgantown, WV. Pastor David M. Hudson leads the church. We walked in and were greeted by the pastor. He showed us to the prayer room. We had a powerful time of prayer. Then we came together with Bishop Hudson and prayed. When we were done praying, the three of us talked a little and cried a little.

Riverside Apostolic Church / Riverside Ministries in Morgantown, WV

All of the events of the past few days had taken a lot out of us (and many others, too). We vowed to stick together and be strong, for each other and Zach, no matter what might happen over the next few days, weeks, or months. We vowed to be there for Zach. As parents, Cheri and I have always instilled in our boys that God is number one, and then family is the next most important aspect of life.

Zach met Tim and Pam Woody, residents of Buckhannon, WV. Pam had been injured and was a patient at HealthSouth. She had been there for three months prior to our arrival. She stayed only a few doors down the hall from Zach's room. An incredible friendship was formed between our two families, so much so that it continues to this day.

Eventually Zach went outside to shoot basketball with Jesse Glaspell, JT Sandy, and friends. I set his wheelchair in front of the basketball hoop, and Zach leaned against it and shot baskets.

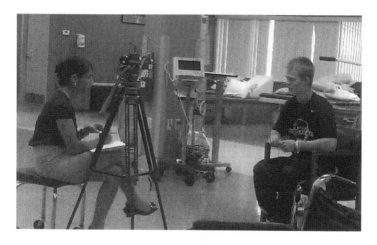

Stacy Jacobson from WBOY TV channel 12, in Clarksburg, WV, called and wanted to do a follow-up story on Zach's miracle. She came and interviewed Zach and me. Cheri was too camera-shy to be interviewed. Zach talked about the challenges he had faced thus far, and what he hoped for the future.

Zach's room was full of cards, posters, candies, brownies, pepperoni rolls, etc. He still had the prayer shawl sent to him from youth at Cornerstone Apostolic

Church in Winchester, VA, where his aunt & uncle, Dave and Brenda Sandy, and their son, Brandon, attend church. He had another blanket from his friend, Cayla Bayles, and a third blanket that other family members had brought to him. Zach struggled to walk while there. He could stand for brief periods, but he used a wheelchair to get around. At times I would have someone get in the wheelchair and let Zach walk behind it and push them to strengthen his legs. Zach would tire quickly, when we would then take him to his room to rest.

Our home church, Christian Apostolic Church in Clarksburg, WV

On Sunday morning, July 22, the Sandy family used one of our iPhones, via its FaceTime app, to watch the live church service going on back home in Clarksburg at Christian Apostolic Church, led by Pastor Doug Joseph. (The prior two days, Zach and family had inquired with the doctors and nurses at HealthSouth about letting Zach go to church Sunday morning. One doctor approved, but then the next morning a social worker came in and burst our bubble; she spoke of insurance policies that would not permit Zach to be gone from the facility for any long period of time.)

We did not get to attend church that morning, but the Bayles family from there in Morgantown came to visit Zach that Sunday evening. They took him in his wheelchair across the street to Applebee's (probably Zach's most favorite place to eat). Zach did not eat much, but he had a smile on his face the whole evening.

Zach was getting restless. He wanted to go home. He still could not walk very well. He had to use a walker and wheelchair if he was going to be on his feet for any length of time. He was still not eating well. We watched his weight spiral downward. He slept a great deal. He was getting frustrated, but he hid it pretty well most of the time. He never complained, although he was anxious.

The last three days at HealthSouth were filled with family and friends stopping in. Visiting hours were 4:00 to 8:30 every evening. Cheri and I actually went back to work on Monday, July 23. Other family members stayed with Zach off and on, until Cheri and I got back there in the evenings. Then once Zach was tucked in at night, Cheri and I went home (about a 35-minute drive) for work the next day.

I remember one of the times when Cheri and I were again driving to HealthSouth—absolutely numb with tiredness. Rusty rode along with us on this particular day. As we stopped to get a drink at the McDonald's in Fairmont, WV, my phone rang just as we were getting out of the car. I did not recognize the number. This was nothing new; our whole family was getting calls from numbers that we did not recognize.

When I answered the phone, I immediately knew who it was. No matter how tired, I would have recognized anywhere the voice of one of our most favorite preachers on earth. The voice on the phone was none other than Pastor Jeff Arnold of Gainesville, Florida. I was stunned and in disbelief that he had called me.

Over and over I said, "No way this is Jeff Arnold."

Finally Brother Arnold interrupted me and said, "OK, it's really Uncle Sam. Give me all your money!"

Brother Arnold went on to tell me that someone had alerted him that my son had suffered a run-in with a bolt of lightning, and he wanted to call and speak words of faith to me. Just a little while before this, Brother Arnold had a marvelous miracle take place in his life. He was preaching at a conference and died right on the platform. God then raised him up. He proceeded to tell me that he felt impressed of God that the person he had called to speak about *was a worshipper.*

Indeed, Zach has never been ashamed to worship God. Brother Arnold then spoke a profound truth to me.

Jeff Arnold said, "Hell cannot stop a worshipper!"

I will forever remember those words. Many thanks go to my brother, David Sandy, for setting up that phone call. That conversation gave me a surge of faith that I personally needed at that moment.

Zach continued to have trouble. He was still not sleeping well, and his appetite was still poor at best. Zach seemed to have pain and restlessness in his legs and hips. The staff at HealthSouth contemplated giving him stronger medicine for pain, but Zach, Cheri and I really did not want to risk him getting started on pain pills. We agreed that he could take over-the-counter medicine for the pain.

Chapter 11:
Coming Home

Wednesday July 25, 2012 (on the twenty-fourth birthday of Zach's older brother, Rusty), Zach got the news he wanted: he was going home! This was exactly two weeks removed from taking somewhere between 20,000 to 60,000 thousand volts of electricity to the top of his head. Hallelujah!

Discharge plans included Zach attending outpatient rehab at a facility closer to home, in Bridgeport, WV, three times per week. Zach got another wish—to stop by Chick-Fil-A restaurant in Morgantown (just down the street from HealthSouth). Zach rode with his friend, Cayla Bayles, in her vehicle. Zach thought he might see a good friend who works at Chick-Fil-A, Pastor David Harris Sr. Zach did get to see him, as Brother Harris was working that day. Pastor Harris reminded Zach that when he first heard of the lightning strike, he was at work and could not find a suitable place to pray, so Brother Harris had locked himself in the restroom to pray there.

A vehicle filled with cards, balloons, posters, etc., carried Zach down I-79, some 44 miles to Stonewood, WV. I remember the ride home as Zach rested. He fell asleep in the passenger seat. I prayed and thanked God for what had taken place in the past two weeks.

I said to myself, "We serve a great, big, wonderful God, but as big as God is, I do not know if He fully realizes how thankful we are to Him for what He has done for my family!"

Driving the last few miles before arriving home, throughout the neighborhood there were several signs cheering Zach on. Then in the Sandy's driveway a barrage of signs and posters greeted him. A few folks had set up a party for Zach to welcome him home. Some refreshments were prepared. Zach was really tired, so he went straight to the couch. We got Zach's room organized and set up a table for refreshments and snacks; a place to get everything Zach would need within one area.

When we returned home from HealthSouth, we found our house stocked with bottled water and Gatorade. Our freezer and refrigerator were both filled. Our cabinets were running over. Our home church, Christian Apostolic Church, had blessed us!

Besides being home at last and trying to pace himself, Zach had one other thing on his mind that would complete "being home." Zach was adamant that he had saved enough energy, and he wanted to go to church!

We took him there. In the church service there was a powerful time of worship. Zach and we, as parents, got to talk a little bit about the past two weeks. Even before Zach's accident, he had a passion for just being in church as much as he could.

Thursday, July 26, one day after coming home from HealthSouth, Zach's pain seemed to get worse. He was in tremendous pain. We decided to take him to the local emergency room. The doctors at United Hospital Center in Bridgeport, WV, were stunned to hear what had happened to him. They consulted Zach's doctor from HealthSouth, Dr. Russell Biundo. Zach was given a stronger medicine that day, which helped with the restlessness and pain in his hip area and legs.

On Saturday, July 28, 2012, a bigger, more public homecoming celebration was held for Zach at the two adjacent homes of Zach's Uncle, John Sandy, and Zach's Mamaw, Helen Sandy.

Both front and back yards, as well as the insides of the homes, were filled with friends, family, and guests, all come to help celebrate Zach's return.

Our heartfelt gratitude goes out to all those who organized the party, including John and Tracy Sandy, my sister, Susan, and others, as well as to all who attended. Many folks showed up at different times.

At the celebration Zach was hurting badly, so he rested on Mamaw's couch for a while. However, he spent a lot of time outside greeting everyone. Zach even joined in a friendly game of "Whiffle Ball" in the backyard. Although it was good to see him standing on his own and holding a bat and swinging, he was still a long way from back to normal.

Pastor Dan Bayles, along with his wife, Courtney, and their kids, attended the party. Cayla Bayles, who has already been mentioned several times, is the oldest daughter of Dan and Courtney. Cayla had received a text from Zach a few weeks after he graduated. A few days before Zach went to Ocean City, Cayla had come to Clarksburg to spend some time with Zach. They had gone to the local mall and had dinner with Cheri and me. Zach and Cayla had texted each other over the following week or so. Cayla and her family had gone to Myrtle Beach for the week of July 9. When the lightning strike occurred, I knew that at some point I had to get word to Cayla's parents. I did not want Cayla to first learn of it via Facebook. Long story short: At the welcome home celebration Zach asked Pastor Bayles if he could talk to him off to the side. Dan obliged, not knowing what was up. Zach asked him if he could ask Cayla to be his girlfriend.

Dan replied, "Well, I think that would be just awesome." (At least that is what Zach remembers him saying.) Zach and Cayla were then officially courting.

The next couple of months were full of pain for Zach, and sleepless nights for Cheri and me. Three times a week he went as an outpatient to United Rehab in Bridgeport, WV. The first few weeks, as a result of the physical therapists stretching his leg muscles and him trying to walk on a treadmill, Zach hurt terribly, mainly in the evenings and overnight. Many nights Cheri and I stayed up with Zach, prayed, and rubbed his legs, trying to lessen the pain. Zach spent several hours in the bathtub after he filled it with hot water.

His Papaw Welch bought him a device that made the water swirl, similar to how a hot tub would function. We bought supports to place around the tub, so Zach could get in and out of it safely. Heating pads and heating blankets were given to Zach, along with a small heater. These were Zach's "best friends" at times. Nana and Papaw Welch, Cissie Cutlip, Mamaw Sandy and a few others spent days with Zach and took him to his rehab appointments. Zach's appetite eventually came back, some thanks to Buffalo Wild Wings and Applebee's restaurants. Zach kept his Bible and notebook close to him at home. He also enjoyed afternoon naps and the TV show "Criminal Minds."

Cheri and I began to look for a small puppy for Zach to help him in his recovery. Many were considered. Some were too big, some too old, some too far away to fetch. Then one day a young lady in our church, Sister Amanda Berry, sent pictures to Zach and Cheri of a puppy that was a Chihuahua & Dachshund mix (sometimes called a Chaweenie). This was the exact puppy they were looking for.

That very night at church, Zach picked up the puppy, and "Daisy" became Zach's new friend. Daisy was a lazy puppy, which was OK. Daisy and Zach spent countless hours on the couch in a daze, or a stupor (a term Zach's

Mamaw Sandy taught him), which means being awake and asleep at the same time.

Daisy had no concept of a potty place. You could take her outside for a walk, bring her back inside, and Daisy would proceed to do her business right in front of the fireplace. I suppose it was more comfortable there than outside. Zach and Cheri tried diligently to train her, but Daisy was stubborn.

Daisy did have some good traits. Zach slept on the couch for a while, so we could hear if he needed help. If we did not hear him, Daisy would come to our room and sit near the bed and whimper until Cheri or I woke up to attend to Zach. If that did not work, Daisy would jump onto the bed and lick Cheri's face until she woke up and checked on Zach.

Back when Zach had been released from HealthSouth they had provided him with a wheelchair and a walker. At home he used the walker to get around. His knees would give out, and he would fall from time to time. Cheri would always get onto Zach when she saw him trying to lean on the furniture to get around.

One day when Zach was napping, he woke with the urge to use the restroom. So he stood up and began to walk to the restroom. Zach had walked 10 to 12 steps before he realized that he had not brought his walker with him. While contemplating what to do, he finished the trip to the restroom and started back to his chair before hearing his mother's words of reprimand.

She demanded to know, "Zach what are you doing? And where is your walker?"

Mom had caught him! He explained that he had just gotten up and started walking. I was not home at the time, but when I heard later what had happened, I took it as good news.

I commented, "God just keeps healing Zach a little at a time, and God is going to finish the healing in His own time."

Family members were so supportive. Several churches sent financial offerings. Some churches held benefit dinners and fundraisers for Zach and his family. An account was set up by some awesome friends, the Henderson family, at a local bank as a place to donate for Zach.

We were very appreciative of every kind gesture and every penny that was given. Several cards were received in the mail with donations and kind, supportive words. Monies were set aside for medical bills and water bills from where Zach was soaking his pains away in hot water in the bathtub, and the electric bills from all the extra heating pads and heaters, etc.

Zach loved to hunt and fish. I got him to the river to fish as often as I could. One day while we were fishing with a friend, Julius Lockett, Zach received a call from George Rath of the KLOVE radio network. He asked Zach and me a few questions each. He was doing a story on Zach's miracle for the radio, to be aired on the Christian network. Pastor Joseph was also interviewed, and the story was later aired on the KLOVE radio website and aired throughout America on all their stations. (KLOVE later did follow up stories. Our thanks go to George Rath and Richard Hunt.)

Zach and I often fished, usually with JT Sandy (Zach's fishing buddy) and Uncle John (JT's dad). Zach's cousins joined us whenever they could. There was a steep hill. One had to walk down to the fishing spot and back up to leave. Zach could not get down or up very well. Julius Lockett literally carried Zach back up the hill once while we were leaving.

Testifying at ministry events, churches, etc.
Zach attended the Azusa StreetRiders (biker ministry) national rally, which (for that year) just happened to be hosted at his home church during August 1-5, 2012. Although he didn't make it every night, one night Zach testified before the whole group. The bikers asked Zach a lot of questions about the accident. During that week one person was filled with the Holy Ghost for their very first time.

Zach visited Brother Brad Glaspell's church (House of the Lord Jesus Christ, in Clarksburg, WV) on Sunday night, August 5, and he spoke about God's miracle.

Zach's Nana Welch and his Aunt Cissie Cutlip had planned to have a booth at that year's "JesusFest" (a regional Christian festival held annually in downtown Clarksburg). On August 11, 2012, they set up a booth at the event, to sell various items to benefit their church. To help us with medical bills, they graciously offered some wristbands and small pictures of Zach for sale. Zach was there, and he met several folks. Some of the event staff came and prayed for Zach.

While at the "JesusFest" event, a lady actually asked Zach for his autograph. Zach was surprised by this request.

With a good humor Zach had replied, "I am not sure why you need my autograph. I didn't do anything. God did this miracle; go get His autograph!"

Zach's presence at the Christian festival was featured in the local newspaper shortly thereafter. (Ever since the ordeal first occurred, Zach has repeatedly been featured in reports in various newspapers, multiple radio stations, several TV channels, and he has been featured in the Internet stories of several major networks. We could not begin to number the blog posts that have been published regarding his testimony.)

Lightning strike victim gets big welcome at Jesus Fest

On Sunday evening, August 19, 2012, Cheri and Zach went to the Liberty Addition Church of God where Zach's Papaw and Nana Welch attend church, and where his Aunt Cissie is the youth pastor. The church blessed Zach tremendously, and Zach spoke of the miracle that God had performed.

We really wanted to get back to Parkersburg to visit. Pastor Ralph Tisdale wanted Zach to come to their church and meet everyone again. So we planned to revisit Parkersburg on August 25-26. We invited family and friends to join us if they wished. Our plan was to see the campground (the site of the lightning strike) on Saturday and revisit the hospital and ambulance service that had taken care of Zach back on July 11. At around 2:00 PM on August 25, 2012, many friends and family gathered at the ball field where the accident happened.

Above: On the ball field on August 25, Zach adopted a posture of praise and thanksgiving to God. This photo (taken by Pastor Doug Joseph) has become yet another iconic image in connection with the miracle.

One month and two weeks after our world had come to a crashing halt, we were standing in the place where Zach had once lain lifeless, totally in the hands of the living God. There was lots of conversation, and Brother Jim Workman and Brother Jesse Glaspell fielded a lot of questions from everyone.

I took the time to walk away from folks a little to talk with God. Emotions were running high for me. I knew it was the same for everyone else there that day. I did not know whether to fall on my face and weep, or give a shout of praise to God for what He had done right there in that open field on July 11. So often you hear of a family returning to the scene of an accident where they lost a loved one. Well, we had lost Zach there a little more than a month prior, yet Zach had come back to us. Thank you, Jesus!

I watched my wife struggle to keep her emotions in check while we were there. A few times she broke down and let her emotions show as Brother Jim and Brother Jesse answered questions. Cheri is a strong woman of God, and she can hide her true emotions at times. However, she is also not afraid to show emotion.

After we had been there for about 20 minutes, the Tisdale family arrived. I quickly introduced everyone to them, and Pastor Doug Joseph asked Pastor Ralph Tisdale to talk a little about what had transpired there. While Pastor Joseph videoed the testimony, Brother Tisdale told the chilling story of lifelessness, CPR, faith, and prayer—all wrapped up in the space of about a half an hour on July 11. Brother Tisdale's comments can be seen in a video on YouTube (just search for "Zach Sandy"). After Brother Tisdale spoke, we joined together in prayer, thankful for God's mighty acts.

We followed through on our plan to visit Camden Clark Memorial Hospital. Only the receptionist remembered us having been there that day. We learned that at one time, the receptionist had lived in North View neighborhood in Clarksburg, WV—near to where my wife and her family had lived. The receptionist actually recognized Cheri and family when she saw them. What a small world! I have said a million times that my wife knows everyone.

None of the doctors or nursing staff that helped Zach back on July 11 were there at the time of our visit. The staff members on hand were gracious enough to let us go back to the room where we first saw Zach. The staff on duty asked us a few questions, and some of them remembered having heard about Zach and the accident. They were all amazed at his progress.

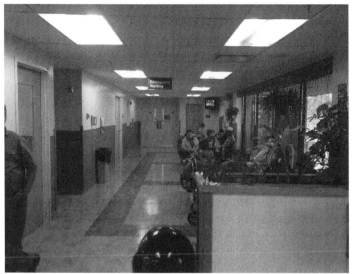

Above: the long hallway and foreboding doors that we had travelled through in a fog of concern back on July 11

Next we walked across the street to the ambulance service's dispatch office and garage. Larry Steohens was there. He remembered the lightning strike call that had gone out. He had not responded to it personally, but he had heard it mentioned by the folks who did respond. He added that one lady who had gone on the call back on that day had departed from the station just before our visit. We spent a few minutes chatting with him, and then we moved on to dinner at Golden Corral. Most everyone that made the trip joined us to eat. We had an awesome time fellowshipping with the Tisdale family.

We were anxiously anticipating the church service the next morning. I gave out cards that read "Spreading Truth Ministries Church" to the cashier, waitress, and salad bar worker, telling them to come the next morning to hear about a miracle. The cashier actually remembered hearing of the lightning strike and knew someone had been hurt. I brought Zach to introduce him to her. She promised to come to church.

With help from Brother Jim Workman, we had been set up with hotel accommodations near Parkersburg for that night. Among those who stayed were Cheri, Zach, myself, Rusty and Hannah Sandy (son and daughter-in-law), John and Tracy Sandy (brother and sister-in-law) and family, my mother, Cheri's mother and father, and Randy and Jesse Glaspell. We had a relaxing time, and Caleb came by to spend time with Zach. Zach and some others went for a swim in the pool. Zach was in pain, so he also spent a little time in the hot tub.

At bedtime, I made the suggestion that Zach sleep in Jesse's room that night. On many nights Cheri and I had taken turns sleeping in a chair next to Zach or doing the half-sleep/half-awake thing all night listening for him or Daisy to let us know he was in pain and needed something.

Jesse and his dad both said, "Sure, he can stay with us." They were in the room next to ours.

I asked, "Are you sure you know what you are getting yourself into?"

Zach did stay with them, and Cheri and I rested well. Randy told me later that he felt so sorry for Zach, as all night long he laid awake and watched Zach weep and wince in pain. He said he kept asking Zach if there was anything he could do.

Zach had answered him just like he answered Cheri and me: "Just pray."

Sunday morning we woke up greatly anticipating the church service. We were going to the very place where Zach had prayed for a testimony "that would blow people's minds"—a life story that folks would scarcely believe. The worship service was awesome. Spreading Truth Ministries Church has an awesome praise and worship team. Brother Caleb Tisdale spoke about the events of July 11; how it changed his life, and how much it affected the rest of the camp that week.

Pastor Ralph Tisdale spoke a few minutes. He greeted our family and introduced me. He requested that I would introduce Zach. I thanked everyone for what they did for Zach that day at the camp. I thanked Caleb and those who were around the scene for not giving up on Zach. I thanked God that He was gracious enough to give our family a miracle.

I introduced Zach, and he had to be helped onto the stage by his brother, Rusty. Zach winced in pain. At that point he was still unable to climb stairs, jump, or run. Zach spoke for about 15 minutes, expressing to everyone there how thankful he was. Pastor Tisdale then spoke for a few minutes about miracles, and he gave an invitation to "come and receive a miracle for yourself." We had looked forward to this weekend, and it did not disappoint. We had a good time with friends, met new friends, and relaxed some.

Later on that same Sunday (August 26, 2012), we attended the evening service at Solid Rock Worship Center, in Oak Hill, WV, where Pastor Greg Hurley is the overseer. Zach was invited to speak and gave his testimony there, in a wonderful and powerful service.

Above: Zach speaking at Solid Rock Worship Center, in Oak Hill, WV

The F.I.S.H. (First I Seek Him) Student Ministries planned a special "Reverb" event at Christian Apostolic Church, which occurred on September 14, 2012. Hundreds had been invited and many people had committed to attend. We looked forward to many of our friends and family members attending to support Zach. Many flyers and posters were distributed. All our friends on Facebook were invited. Several folks had expressed to us that they wanted to know when Zach was going to tell of this great miracle, and they were notified.

At the event there was a high level of expectancy and faith. There was a charge in the atmosphere. Many friends and family members showed up, in addition to the Leasure family from Parkersburg, WV, Tim and Pam Woody from Buckhannon, WV, accompanied by their pastor, Tim Lewis. Also Regina, a co-worker of mine at United Hospital Center, was there.

In all, about 181 people were in attendance on that magical night when Zach officially began telling his miracle testimony. There were many visitors, some from other assemblies in the area. Extra chairs had to be added to the seating in the sanctuary. Zach's friend, Cayla Bayles, came with her family. Her dad, Daniel Bayles, is pastor of Calvary Apostolic Church in Uniontown, PA. Cayla and her youth group's sign team worshipped to the song, "Power In the Name of Jesus." The song's lyrics speak of healing in the name of Jesus, and salvation in the name of Jesus. Somewhere near the end of the song, Zach appeared from the back of the stage to signify that a miracle had taken place.

Pastor Doug Joseph spoke of miracles. He mentioned that back on the day of the lightning strike, he had just concluded a meeting with the West Virginia UPCI district board in Charleston, WV, and had just gotten on the road back to Clarksburg when they were informed of the accident. He recounted their fervent prayers and desperate efforts to get to where Zach was located. He pointed out that Zach was the beneficiary of an even greater miracle than having been raised from the dead: some 10 years earlier, Zach had been baptized with the Holy Ghost with the evidence of speaking in tongues, and had received remission of sins through repentance and water baptism in Jesus name! In light of eternity, salvation is always a higher priority than any physical healing.

Pastor Brad Glaspell spoke of his drive to Parkersburg with Zach, prior to the lightning strike. He mentioned how impressed he was by Zach's goals for his life and by his hunger to grow closer to God. Brad also commented that whenever all those prayers had gone up for Zach, God already knew who Zach was. God had heard that name before, because Zach was truly a dedicated child of God.

Lindsay Leasure-Kupfner also spoke for a few minutes, telling of how she and her mother, Sandy Leasure, had heard the call go out. Lindsay said that they instantly ran to their car and drove to the camp where the accident had taken place. She said it was a horrific scene, but she did not hesitate before offering assistance. She helped with CPR, assisting Caleb. Lindsay indicated that she would never forget Zach's beautiful blue eyes contrasted against a scene of tragedy.

Above: My wife and I addressed the crowd at the Reverb event, themed as a "Time for Miracles." God anointed testimonies of Zach's miracle.

Cheri and I spoke for a few minutes, thanking everyone over and over for all the help and support. Both of us told about how we were notified that Zach had been hit by lightning. Sudden disbelief and horror were instantaneously replaced by faith and trust in the almighty God. We both reflected that you never think that your own family will ever go through something such as this; it is always "the Jones" family down the road that experiences these types of things. There is no way to prepare for something like this, but it is utterly overwhelming to have support from family, church family, community, and even more places than you would ever expect to see offer love and help.

Zach was given the floor. He took the microphone and rehearsed the events of July 11 and the month or so that followed. I knew Zach was in real pain that night, but he spoke like a champion. Zach acknowledged, quite humorously, that every time he tells his testimony 75% of it is hearsay because he was unconscious when most of the events of July 11 took place. Zach spoke for about 20 minutes, and when he handed the microphone back to his pastor, tears were flowing from just about everyone's eyes.

Pastor Joseph gave a call for folks to come and receive their own miracle, not only for healing, but also for the greatest miracle of all, salvation. Many visitors came to pray, with one person receiving the baptism of the Holy Ghost with the evidence of speaking in tongues.

The next day, Saturday, September 15, 2012, we drove to Martinsburg, WV, to spend the night with David and Brenda Sandy and their son, Brandon. We were invited to come to their church, Cornerstone United Pentecostal Church, in Winchester, VA, the following day. We had a good time on Saturday. Zach couldn't do much, so we paced ourselves. He was hurting badly most of the day. Night fell, and we were excited for church the next day. On Sunday morning at 8:00, my brother, David, received a call from a local television station saying they wanted to come and do a story on the miracle.

We arrived at the church, and Pastor Dillon greeted us at the door. The TV station was ready to interview Zach, Cheri, and me right before church. We went outside for the interview; I suggested that we stand so the church sign would be directly behind us as we spoke—free advertising for the church! The reporter filmed some of the church service and some of Zach's testimony.

We feel at home every time we go to Cornerstone UPC. Winchester and the surrounding area is so blessed to have an awesome place to go and worship God. The people are very kind and compassionate. It was a fantastic service. Zach spoke for a while, and later the young kids, who had sent him the prayer shawl while he was in West Penn Hospital, all anointed him in prayer. The church blessed Zach tremendously. After the church service, both Sandy families had lunch with Pastor and Sister Dillon at Cracker Barrel Restaurant.

Brother Dillon spoke words of wisdom to me at the table—words that stick with me yet today.

Many requests came in for Zach to tell his testimony in front of organizations and congregations. I became the secretary for Zach and his travels, fielding calls from all over. We paced ourselves at first, knowing that Zach's health and rest were of top priority.

The miracle continues to touch lives every time Zach or anybody else tells about it.

Deer Hunting

By November of 2012 Zach was still not getting around very well. The third week of November has always been one of Zach's favorite times of the year.

When both boys were young I had taken them hunting, as my Dad had done for me. I felt that I should teach them to respect the outdoors and to know firearm safety and proper use, again as my Dad had done for me. Rusty liked to go, but I am not sure he was overjoyed about it. Zach, on the other hand, loved it from the start. Zach was so excited that he had started cleaning the rifles way back in July to prepare for that November's deer season.

Zach had been given two bows, and he had fixed them up. He and I had gotten to bow hunt a couple of times at Brad Glaspell's hunting area.

The first morning of deer season, Zach and I arrived at Brad's about 6:00 AM. Brad took us on the hill at about 6:30 AM. (Brad had a Kubota four-wheeler, and he took Zach and me up on the hill in it. Zach would not have been able to climb that hill, otherwise.) Brad had set up a table and chairs for Zach, and we took blankets to wrap around Zach's legs. (The colder his legs got, the more they ached and hurt.) Zach and I sat in the dark for about 25 minutes. We could hear something moving in the woods about 75 yards away. There was not yet enough daylight for us to see well, so we just waited. As the day dawned, we could see that there was a deer just inside the wood line off to our left. We waited patiently for the deer to come into the right-of-way.

About 7:00 AM, when we could finally see well, Zach said, "There he is. It is a buck."

I replied, "Get a good look at him, and take him down."

A few seconds later Zach squeezed the trigger, and the deer was Zach's. It was a seven-point buck. The rack was not huge, but Zach didn't seem to care. He had gotten his buck! All of it had been made possible by the big, kind heart of Brad Glaspell. I thanked Brad over and over for truly going out of his way to make hunting possible for my son.

Chapter 12:
The Sky is the Limit

ach has been to many places telling his testimony at several churches and organizations. Zach spoke at the Clarksburg Mission to a packed house at their downtown facility. Zach and family have traveled as far as King George, VA, about six hours away.

No matter where Zach has gone, one part of his testimony is always consistent: he wants no credit of his own. He says over and over that he did nothing; God did it all. God gets all the credit.

From hearts full of gratitude, we want to thank all who helped on July 11 and during the following months. Thank you, Caleb Tisdale and Lindsay Leasure. Thanks to all of the paramedics that responded that day: Lori Fulton Short, Jim Lemley, Shawn McKenna, and one or two others we haven't met yet. Thanks to all the medical personnel at all four facilities where we have been over these few months.

On May 4, 2013, we finally got to meet two of the special people that responded on July 11: Lori Short and Jim Lemley. In Parkersburg, we met with them as well as Caleb Tisdale, and the Leasure family. Zach presented each one of these genuine heroes with two red roses and a plaque.

As of the time of this printing (June 2013), Zach's physical abilities have grown to the place where now he is able to jog, and when he wants to praise the Lord in the dance during a great church service, he can do just that. Zach is a worshipper, and he always has been. Regaining his mobility for praising God means more to him than any athletic ability he might regain.

Final thoughts
From Cheri and me as parents, looking back on the past nine months, we are grateful and indebted for all the prayers. We know that several folks have prayed for Zach for a healing, and they prayed for us to be strong for Zach. We are thankful to family and friends that were right by our side the whole time. We are thankful for all of the donations, kind words, and kind gestures.

It is very likely that we have unintentionally omitted quite a few of the many kind things that folks did for us. We apologize in advance. That does not mean that it was not appreciated.

During several of the TV, radio, and newspaper interviews, we have stressed to the viewers, listeners and readers the following important priorities: love your kids, and let your kids know every day that you love them. Even when you have to discipline them, make sure they know why you are doing it. As a man, I have observed that so very often females outdo us guys, usually by having the "Mom" effect. Mothers love unconditionally. Fathers usually deal out the discipline, whether it be grounding, or taking a phone away. Men, you must be the "Father" and set the rules and regulations of the home, but there are also times when you *must* be the "Dad," and love your kids unconditionally, just like Mom.

Without a doubt, our boys always knew how both of us felt about them. We had prayed together and talked all the time. We knew they loved us. When Zach had been lying there lifeless, we already knew how he felt about us. Zach was also loved by his brother, Rusty, his sister-in-law, Hannah, and by his Mamaw, Papaw and Nana Welch, and all of his aunts and uncles, cousins, and church family. If tragedy ever strikes in your life, don't let it sever your tie without you having expressed your love!

Cheri and I have stressed to several folks that if you have a long-standing fight with one of your kids, or you have not spoken with them for a period of time, please contact them and make things right. Life is too short to fuss and feud with your own flesh and blood!

Whenever something traumatic happens, people begin to talk about "putting things into perspective." You realize then that some things matter, and in turn some things simply do not matter. The truly wise person will keep all things in proper perspective even before a traumatic event occurs.

Cheri, Zach and I have been faithful to church for a long time. In fact we often visit other churches as well (such as when we are out of town) just to be in church. We also try to attend every fellowship meeting and church conference that our schedules will allow. God honors faithfulness!

Cheri, Zach and I now celebrate the eleventh day of each month. Zach now has three birthdays: his natural birthday, his spiritual birthday, and his "miracle birthday." Often we all watch the videos on the CAC website and on YouTube. We talk about the whole ordeal often.

Many of the interview videos and the awesome videos that Pastor Doug Joseph put together can be viewed on our church website at cac.wvupci.com/zach or on our publisher's website at whitestonepublishing.com/zach or by going to YouTube and searching for "Zach Sandy."

Once the right perspective has been obtained (often won by a hard fight) it must not be allowed to slip! May God bless you with a good sense of perspective.

Appendix: Testimonials

The following are individual testimonials from family, friends, former coaches, and folks that Zach and his family have met through this event. Enjoy.

Cayla Bayles:
The week of July 11 my family and I were on vacation at the beach. I had just come inside from spending the day near the ocean, and I checked my phone to see if Zach had texted me. The last message he had sent me was, "Cayla, you there?" I texted him back, and then I took a shower. I missed a call from Morgan Hurley, but I thought I'd call her back later. Then my brother, Jordan, told me that Zach had been struck by lightning. I didn't know yet how serious the situation was. I called Morgan as soon as I could, and she told me what had happened to Zach. I was terrified. I ran down to the beach and told my parents what happened. We all joined hands and prayed for Zach. As soon as we got home from vacation, my Dad took me to the West Penn Burn Center in Pittsburgh to see Zach.

I know Zach has been changed through this whole event, but I have also been changed. My faith has grown tremendously. I thank God every day for the miracle He performed that day and for the miracle He's performing every day. I have no doubt in my mind now that our God can do absolutely anything!

Zach, God is healing you more and more each day. I've watched you heal ever since that tragic day. It's amazing! God has proved that He is almighty, and He has everything in his hands. He has a plan for everything. I'm so very blessed that God brought you into my life. Being here for you through everything has changed my life in an amazing way. I admire you for being so strong and always keeping your trust in God. Not very many people could go through such a life-changing event and still keep believing that God has everything in control. I believe that He will heal you completely. I will always be by your side, and I will keep praying for you every day. You mean so much to me! Keep on trusting God! You're the best!

Love,
Cayla Bayles

Helen "Mamaw" Sandy

On July 11, 2012, I was in Georgia visiting with my daughter, Linda, and her family. My grandson, JT, was with me. I was in the living room with JT and Linda's youngest son, Landon. Suddenly my son-in-law, Ashley, rushed through the door and told the boys to leave the room. I could hear in his voice that something was wrong.

Ashley told me, "Zach was in an accident."

Instantly I asked, "Whose car was he in?"

Ashley told me, "He was not in a car. He was struck by lightning, and he is not responding."

I was in total shock, and I panicked, saying, "Oh, God, please do not take my Zach." I said it over and over. Ashley tried to calm me down.

Linda was on her way home from work. When Linda arrived she began to read from a book she had, using Zach's name over and over. Such a calmness came over me. I knew that Zach had been called into the ministry a few years back, and I knew God was in control. Zach always went to church. He was such a good person. I knew God had plans for his future. Then we heard news that he had a pulse. It was great to hear. Thank you, Jesus!

We left the next morning and drove to Pittsburgh where Zach was, praying as we journeyed on. We got to the Burn Center, and lots of family and friends were there. I got to go in and see Zach. Thank You, Jesus, for Your healing power!

I got to spend a few days there with family and friends, so I could be close to Zach.

Teresa Thomas took me to her house a few nights, then back the next morning. Every time I saw Zach, he was doing much better and looked better as well. Everyone was praying for him for complete healing. After therapy he came home.

I enjoyed so much the days I spent at his house, and now I thank God that Zach is going to college, driving, just being the normal Zach.

This has changed my whole outlook on life. Zach is special to me. Lots of things that they said he would never do, he can do. Praise to God. I enjoy hearing him preach, and I love watching him shout and dance as he praises God. I love that boy named Zach.

"And we know that all things work together for good to them that love God, to them who are the called according to his purpose" (Romans 8:28).

Papaw and Nana Welch

March 18, 1994, was a very special day for us. Our third grandchild was born way ahead of time, due to complications. Zach was designated as a stressed baby. After a few days in the hospital we were all able to breathe a sigh of relief, as he began to respond.

Zach loved his pacifiers. He hid them all over the house, so he could get to them quickly. He was content when he had one in his hand and another in his mouth.

On July 11, 2012, at 2:45 PM our lives were forever changed. There are not words to describe how you feel when you receive a phone call that your healthy, fun-loving grandchild was struck by lightning and was dead.

Our first response was to run to the Rock of our Salvation, Jesus. So we began to call upon Him, and a sweet peace swept over us. We then began to speak life into Zach. Somehow we knew God wasn't finished with him yet. After some 30 minutes we received another call that the EMTs had a pulse, and Zach was on the way to the hospital. We were in route to Parkersburg, also. Within six hours, Zach was in three different hospitals, and he had been on two ambulance rides by road and another by helicopter. We thank God that He is faithful and He rewards faithfulness. It has been a continual journey with many miracles along the way. We claimed a miracle every time we heard a negative report, and we did not allow those reports to take root. Thank You, God, for Your miracles and for Zach. All that Zach has been through has only strengthened us and caused us to lean on God. We love you, Zach.

Rusty Sandy (Zach's brother)
My day started at 5:40 AM on July 11, 2012. I was working that morning in the grill area at UHC (United Hospital Center). I worked until 2:10 PM. I realized that the next shift's grill worker was going to have a heavy workload. So I asked the supervisor if I could stay over an hour to help him. I'm glad I did stay over as well. After I had finished with helping, I saw that my phone showed four missed phone calls and two voicemails. I looked to see who had called me. My Mom and Dad had called me. So I immediately called for my Dad, and I got him.

I asked, "Dad, what is wrong?" I could tell from the sound of his voice that something was terribly wrong.

He told me, "Zach has been struck by lightning. He's not responding. He's not breathing." He continued and said, "Oh, Lord, please don't take Zach! Take me!"

I spoke to my dad in faith: "Dad, don't talk like that; everything is going to be all right." My Dad told me where they were transporting him. I got in my car and started the drive to Lowe's, where my wife, Hannah, worked. On the way, I called her.

As soon as I got her on the phone, she said, "Where are you?"

I said, "I'm on Interstate-79."

She said, "Your Dad already called me. Meet me at the Lowe's parking lot." My dad had called Hannah to tell her what had happened, because I did not hear my cell phone earlier. I arrived at the Lowe's parking lot and we proceeded to make the trip to Camden Clark Memorial Hospital in Parkersburg, WV. My wife decided it was wise that she drive because I was in no condition to drive. I was praying and having faith during the drive.

During one point of the trip my phone rang. It was my Dad.

He said, "They have a pulse." My wife and I rejoiced in the car together. We did not make it to Camden Clark Memorial Hospital. My dad had confirmed to me that Zach was being transported to Ruby Memorial Hospital in Morgantown, WV. So my wife and I turned around to begin the trip to Ruby Hospital in Morgantown, WV. At that point in time I just wanted to see my brother.

We arrived at Ruby Memorial Hospital. The waiting room was filled with people, many friends and family. While we waited for the ambulance to arrive, I remember noticing that it was a great show of strong support. We are blessed to have a great family and great friends. Shortly after our arrival to Ruby Memorial Hospital, my Mother and Uncle John arrived. Mom showed me Zach's burned-and-melted clothes, shoes damaged by the lightning, and a cell phone that was destroyed by the strike.

Finally, Zach's ambulance arrived. My Dad got out of the passenger side of the ambulance, and I met him with a big hug. The paramedics were getting ready to bring Zach out of the ambulance.

I said to myself, "I have to say something to my brother when he goes by on a stretcher." So I thought of something he would have said to me if he was standing here and I was on the stretcher. As he went by I said, "Be strong, Z, be strong!"

My brother and I have had this close bond ever since I can remember. We talked with each other about everything. Nothing was hidden from each other. It was hard for me because I wasn't able to talk to my brother about this until after he woke up. Later, I was able to go back and see him in the emergency room

While we were there at Ruby Memorial Hospital, at one point everyone that was there gathered in a big circle out on the lawn, and we all prayed for Zach. It was powerful to see. Afterward the doctors confirmed that they would be sending him to the West Penn Burn

Center in Pittsburgh, PA. So Mom, Dad, Uncle John, Aunt Tracy, myself, and my wife made the drive to Pittsburgh, PA. The nurses were very kind to let us come and see him as we wanted. We knew the whole time that God had His hand on Zach.

On Thursday, after they had taken him off the breathing machine, Zach looked at me and said, "Bubby, will you get me a Gatorade?"

Zach always enjoyed Gatorade. God had His hand on Zach the whole entire time. I'm so blessed to know that Zach Sandy is still alive today! God is *still* in the miracle working business!

John Sandy (Zach's uncle)

Zach has always been like one of our own children. I work midnight shift, so on Wednesday morning, July 11, 2012, I came home and went to bed, as usual. Sometime in the early afternoon hours (I guess around 2:45 PM) my daughter woke me.

She said, "Dad, Zach has been struck by lightning, and Uncle Bud [aka Zach's dad] needs you to call him."

Not fully realizing the impact of what had happened, and not really being fully awake, I didn't really respond much, so she repeated, "Uncle Bud needs you to call him."

I dialed my brother's cell, but the line was busy. I laid my head on the pillow and waited a minute or two, still not really grasping the severity of what was happening with Zach two hours away from us in Parkersburg. I dialed again, and when he finally answered, I could immediately hear the trauma in his voice. I rose up in bed as he spoke words I'll never forget.

Bud said, "John, Zach was struck by lightning and is unresponsive."

I immediately began getting dressed as we spoke on the phone. Bud and Cheri were at Cheri's place of work, just a half-mile from my house. Within minutes of being awakened, I made it there to drive them to Parkersburg. (I knew they were in no condition to drive.)

We were definitely moving faster than the posted speed limit on what would still seem like the longest journey I've ever driven. As Bud and Cheri prayed and called friends for prayer, I drove and prayed, praying in tongues, mostly, because I couldn't find words for what we were feeling. Yet, even with the uncertainty of what was happening, there seemed to be a sense of "God is in control."

We had made it a good distance on Route 50 when the call finally came that they had "found a pulse!"

Bud had answered the phone call with "Brad, give me good news...." Seconds later, after Brad told him there was a pulse, I heard Bud say, "That's all God needs. He has taken over!"

It still seemed like forever before we got there, but we arrived at the hospital in Parkersburg. Pastor Ralph Tisdale met us in the parking lot. Jim Workman and a few others met us in the lobby, as we passed by to find Zach.

The first sight was horrifying. Zach lay motionless, attached to numerous machines and instruments, but still we felt a sense of calm because, "God is in control."

In the next two days we would witness firsthand the miracle working power of God. Zach, of course, was moved from Parkersburg to Morgantown by ambulance, and then to the West Penn Burn Center in Pittsburgh by helicopter. My wife and I stayed with Zach's parents and other family members for the next couple of days.

When we arrived at the West Penn Burn Center the doctor's told us that the "bruise" looking marks on Zach's body were actually burns. We were told that Zach's body was burning from the inside out, and those marks would get worse for the next few days and get pretty gross looking as they "burn outward." The next morning (Thursday, the day after being struck by lightning) Zach's burns had not worsened any at all, but rather started to turn pink as they were healing!

Throughout the day Thursday, the nurses/doctor would come out and tell us signs they were looking for to determine whether or not Zach had incurred any brain damage or muscle damage. When they would tell us what they were looking for, we would pray and even post on Facebook for friends to pray, and within only an hour or two of prayer taking place, God did it! "God is in control."

It has been a life-changing experience for me to be able to see firsthand this miracle from God and to know that "God is in control."

Sky Kase (reporter)
I am a reporter for WTAP, and I covered Zach's story right after it happened. He is a strong, resilient fighter who has made great strides. Zach, I wish you a lifetime of good and happiness.

Joey Lopez-Romano (friend of the family)
The devil tried to destroy the Sandy family, but he did not succeed. Instead, a *miracle* happened on this day. Zach was *dead* after being struck by lightning. With so many prayers and hands upon him, he actually started breathing again. The devil was defeated. Zach is doing

well now and will continue giving *God* the love, honor and praise He deserves!

Brandon Sandy (Zach's cousin)
I was sitting against the wall at the Virginia District UPCI Campground, when my youth pastor, Zane Wells, rushed over and handed me his cell phone.

He said, "It's your Dad." Why didn't he call my phone? Well, because it was dead, as always. As soon as Dad told me the news, I went and told Samuel and some good friends of ours. Not until after I had told them did the realization dawn that my cousin—a brother in the Lord and one of my best friends—may die today. Immediately I went to prayer. After Samuel and I had prayed with one of the greatest families I have ever had the pleasure of meeting (the Hurley family), we went to a wide-open field and prayed and connected with God until they called all the campers into the chapel. By that time I was in total shock. The minister told everyone what happened and we began to pray. Like the church in Acts 12 did for Peter, we prayed without ceasing. As I rushed to the altar I felt God in a mighty way. I could just feel the faith rising like I have never felt before. It turned out to be one of the greatest prayer meetings I have ever been in. Throughout this time of praying the Spirit impressed upon me to repeatedly say this prayer: "Lord, Your work here is not finished."

After that powerful prayer meeting I looked up, and there, on the back wall of the chapel, was a banner that said, "I am the way, the truth, and the life" (John 14:6).

I just smiled and said, "Yes, Lord." At that moment I knew everything was going to be all right, because God is the life. I thank God every day for His grace and mercy, and that He breathed the breath of life into Zach that day. *Keep strong, Zach!*

Samuel Vaughn (cousin to Zach and Brandon)
That poor lizard didn't have a chance. Between my cousin, Zach Sandy, from West Virginia, and myself, we had a green wooden hammer and a plastic screwdriver to combat the beast. We felt accomplished once we had smashed it a good bit. Though we were only three years old at the time, that adventure describes the camaraderie we still share today. Fifteen years later, we've moved on from beating lizards to more practical things like basketball and, yes, girls.

This past summer, I had anticipated attending the West Virginia UPCI youth camp, along with Zach and several of my other cousins and friends. The day before, however, they canceled it due to downed power lines. At the last minute, some friends offered to drive my sister and another cousin of mine, Brandon, to the Virginia District UPCI camp. Unfortunately, Zach couldn't go because he was supposed to start a new job at the hospital that Thursday. We left that Tuesday morning with aspirations of miracles that would take place in our lives.

At 3:00 PM on July 11, 2012, Brandon and I had just finished a basketball tournament, which we lost in an inglorious fashion, and were sitting in the gym. His youth pastor ran up to him and said he had a call from his dad.

Brandon took the call and then looked at me and said, "Zach was struck by lightning."

According to the light-hearted mood, I answered, "Well, good for him."

The blood drained from his face as he replied, "No, Zach was actually struck by lightning." I ran outside and found my sister. We immediately began praying with a group of friends, and after that I made a few phone calls, asking friends to pray. I turned around and saw Brandon walking out into a field. With emotions running high, and my world falling apart, I followed him. We spent about 15 minutes with our faces in the grass, travailing and pleading before God that He would perform a miracle.

The camp administrators called an assembly in the chapel, and about 280 Virginia campers began to speak in tongues and lay hands on Brandon and me, interceding on Zach's behalf. While we were praying,

Brandon's youth pastor got on his bullhorn and announced that the paramedics had found a pulse. At that very moment, covered in sweat and tears, I produced a smile. I can't explain it. It was a peace and joy that I had never felt before. Even though there were a million things that could still go wrong, I knew at that moment that God was in control.

Along with my sister and Brandon's family, I arrived at the hospital in Pittsburgh that Thursday evening. By that time, Zach had been awake for a couple of hours, and he immediately recognized me. When he first awoke, he asked his father to pray and for a hamburger. Three days after being struck dead by lightning, Zach began physical therapy for walking. His charm and goofy personality had returned as he joked about the cute nurses. Besides some short-term memory loss and difficulty walking around, Zach was perfectly fine. In fact, he had no extensive burns on his body. His internal organs cleared their tests, and he was only given minor doses of pain medication due to his miraculous lack of pain.

Today, Zach gives all the glory to God. According to the circumstance, Zach should be taking his rest six feet under the ground. Instead, he is alive and well, traveling to churches across Virginia and West Virginia while sharing his testimony. His doctors even concede that there is no explanation for his recovery other than a miracle. Two months later, he is experiencing restless nights and can't climb steps without assistance. Although he is expected to make a full recovery, he and his family covet your prayers. He had prayed for a miracle, and God responded.

Another amazing quality about Zach is that he had signed to play football with a West Virginia college. A few months before his ordeal he changed course, declining the football scholarship in order to pursue his call into the ministry.

Though I have been taught these principles my entire life without understanding them, this ordeal has taught me three things in particular: God hears and answers prayer; He is a present help in time of trouble; and there is a peace that passes all understanding. I've also adopted a new saying: "But God!" I'm just thankful that I have my friend around to trample lizards for a little while longer. God be praised.

Rev. Ashley and Linda Vaughn (Zach's uncle & aunt)
My name is Ashley Vaughn. My wife, Linda, is Bud's sister and Zach's aunt. On Wednesday, July 11, 2012, I was eager to finish my workday so that I could spend time with my family. My mother-in-law, Helen Sandy, and my nephew, JT Sandy, were visiting with us in our home in Watkinsville, GA. Around 3 o'clock, I received a phone call from Bud, as many times I do. I answered expecting to engage in general conversation,

but that was not the case. Bud told me that Zach had been struck by lightning and was unresponsive.

He said, "Please get to where my mother is." You never know what you will do in this situation, so I told Bud I would get to where she was. We knew there was a chance that she may not survive such tragic news. We determined to do our best to provide peace while breaking it to her. I also told Bud that God was able to handle this. Upon arriving home, Linda and I told Mom what had happened. Yes, I feared the worst for her. You know you believe in the power of God and His peace, but this is where it all comes together.

Would Zach survive? Would my mother-in-law survive? And, if so, how will we have enough peace to handle this? Well, the answer was yet to be seen. However, upon hearing the news, there was this amazing peace unlike anything I've ever experienced. I thought, "Well, this is where we find out if God is really real." As we prayed, the true agony and distress that my mother-in-law experienced was pushed back by the very presence of God. It was as if He was literally there in our living room. I realized that we must prepare to travel, by car, to wherever Zach was. Not knowing where he would finally be, we decided to wait until morning to leave.

As we packed our clothes for this trip, I faced an unexpected dilemma. What do I pack? Do I pack everyday clothes? Then, the reality of packing a suit and tie was... there was a chance that we would be attending a funeral. Standing at my closet, I understood that this could go either way. As we departed and began the 12-hour journey to the Burn Center in Pittsburgh, the emotions were real. In situations of tragedy or extreme sickness, the patient seemingly always improves, yet then worsens. It's always up and down, touch and go. Certainly, this would be no different. We figured that with each call from the family, the reports would either be really good or really bad. This is what I have always experienced. This time something was different. From the first call from Bud, every call that we received in that 24-hour period was of steady improvement, not even one bad report.

By the time we reached Pittsburgh, 24 hours had already passed. Zach Sandy went from dead to definitely alive. Upon our arrival at the hospital, we were greeted with the news that he was awake, talking, praying and healing. A 3-inch wide burn strip down the entire length of his back was already clearing up. You see, Zach was not only alive, but defying all medical protocol. The wonderful staff at the Burn Center was not accustomed to having mobile patients. Usually injuries are so severe that they are not able to move, much less get out of bed. However, Zach was no routine case, for he was dead, yet now alive. At all times, Zach had to have someone at his bedside, not to nurse his injuries, but to keep him in the bed.

As I sat with him the second night, Bud called and said that he faced fear that Zach would never completely heal. I quoted to him Colossians 2:10, "And ye are complete in Him, which is the head of all principality and power."

I said, "Zach will be completely healed." Meanwhile, Zach insisted on exiting his bed. So, guess what? They kicked him out of that hospital and sent him home.

To hear this story from a distance, you might say, "Well, I don't know if all that happened to Zach Sandy. It sounds too good to be true." My only answer to you would be this: It's a God thing. He was truly dead, now he is truly alive. It's amazing what God can do.

Madelyn Vaughn (Zach's cousin)

I was playing a simple game of Bible charades when my older brother and cousin came around the corner looking as pale as ghosts. When they told me that Zach had been struck by lightning, nothing else mattered; I knew we needed to pray. We immediately gathered in a circle with some others and cried out to our God. In just a matter of minutes, the entire camp gathered in the chapel to pray with faith believing that Jesus would come through for us.

The room was filled with young people begging God to restore life to my cousin when somebody said over a bullhorn, "Zach Sandy has a heartbeat!" Everyone threw their hands up and thanked God for his miracle.

The next day we got a ride to the hospital where Zach was. He didn't have any serious burns from the lightning strike! The only noticeable things on Zach were that he had a dark streak down his spine and some burn marks on his feet where the lightning traveled and exited his body. We are so very excited to say that he is back to himself and that all the glory is due to our miracle-working God!

Landon Vaughn (Zach's cousin, currently age 9)
It was July 11, 2012, and my parents, my cousin, my grandmother and I were hanging out together for a week. All of a sudden Dad received a call from Uncle Bud saying that my cousin, Zach, had been struck by lightning. He also said that it was 20,000-40,000 volts of electricity that had ripped through his body. When my dad told my grandmother the news, she couldn't believe what she had heard. She panicked, so my cousin and me tried our best to calm her down. He was struck by lightning on a softball field at a Youth Camp in West Virginia. I was so shocked from what I heard.

The next morning we all had to go to Pittsburgh, PA Burn Center. In the waiting room there were tons of family members and people that knew Zach. We stayed there until the weekend was over. Finally, when I got to go in the room, I saw that Zach had big burns on his back and feet. I never thought I would ever see Zach in a hospital. Finally, about three weeks later, he started to walk, run and jump. I was so happy that my cousin was saved by God.

Note: Many thanks to Landon! While at the West Penn Burn Center, Landon went to folks repeatedly and gave back massages in the waiting room. He would ask for some change each time. At some point before his family departed, Landon presented to Zach the cup of change that he had collected. Landon was eight years old at the time.

The Channel Family, Christian Apostolic Church

We will never forget. It was our wedding anniversary. I was working the nightshift, so I was sleeping at that moment. My wife got a phone call from Sister Cheri that Zach had been struck by lightning. She awakened me. That news was quite a shock. After getting my bearings, we knew that prayer was needed, but we also knew that we had to get to where he and his family needed us. After calling my mother (who had already heard about someone being struck by lightning while she was at a Parkersburg doctors office with my grandmother), she told me of a prayer that was prayed by someone there with them that was the most beautiful prayer they had ever heard. It would turn out to be a long day, but it was just mind-boggling to see the beginning of a miracle that would change Zach so much and to see God put in him a no-fear mentality to preach the word and give his testimony. The Sandy family showed unbreakable faith that we as a family aspire to have one day. I thank God for letting us be friends. Praise the Lord!

Lindsay Leasure-Kupfner
Blue eyes. That was my first impression of Zach. Little did I know I would learn so much more about this great guy in the next few months after his life changed on July 11, the day I met him. People come into our lives for a reason; however, I soon came to realize God put Zach and his entire family in my path to become lifelong friends. Zach is such an inspiration to me as well as so many others. He has so much life ahead of him, and I feel honored to have the opportunity to watch him grow into the reputable young man he has already become. Zach, we all love you like our own family, and I thank God that He brought us to you on that frightful day. It not only changed your life for the better, but mine as well!

Brother Dave & Sister Diana Todd, Cubby, and Austin, Christian Apostolic Church
Zach, we learned about you being struck by lightning through email and Facebook. We read that you may not live, and that was hard for us to believe. With tears

in all of our eyes, we went into prayer. Cubby and
Austin were deeply affected by this; they were also
praying. Whenever they would go do something, they'd
come right back and ask, "How is Zach? Is he ok?" You
and your family mean a lot to us, so we thank God for
each time you can witness of your experience and touch
people's lives, but most of all we're thankful that we can
still hug you and know we are hugging our Miracle
Brother. We serve an awesome God. We love you so
very much.

Note: Cubby and Austin were able to raise over
$100.00 for Zach's hospital bills. Thank you,
boys. You have huge hearts!

Jimmy and Renee Bargo, Christian Apostolic Church
We will never forget the day we received the news
about Zachary being struck with lightning. We were in
the car going to an appointment in Fairmont. Cheri
called our cell, and she was crying.

She said, "Please pray for Zach. He was struck with
lightning." I told her that we would pray and we loved
them. We immediately prayed right there in the car.
We prayed and prayed. I felt peace, and we continued
on to our appointment. I was so unfocused through the
appointment because of wanting to know more details
about Zach and continuing to pray for God to perform
a miracle. We reminded God of the faithfulness of the
Sandy family. We wondered why this was happening.

Well, we continued on the journey with Zach and his family, and we watched an awesome miracle unfold! We're so proud of Zach for his obedience to God and using this horrifying experience to show others about God's awesome love and power! We love you, Zach, and Sandy family! God is using you to touch others, and my faith increases every time I hear the awesome testimony of Zach Sandy!

Brandon Kroll (teammate from RCB baseball team)
Zach is one of my best friends, and when I heard what had happened, I was devastated. I prayed every night for the Lord to heal fully and quickly, and I still pray for that. He is one of the strongest people I know, and it is not hard for me to believe that he is recovering so quickly. The man is a walking miracle, and I see why God decided to touch him. His faith is unparalleled by anyone I have ever met, and he is a terrific young man. I am blessed to have him in my life, and anyone who has met him must feel the same.

Andrea Puckett (friend from VA Camp)
When I found out about Zach, I was terrified. It was very scary to think about. You really don't hear too often about someone getting struck by lightning.

I was at church camp in Virginia when they announced what happened. A few moments later, everyone gathered in the chapel, and we all prayed and interceded for Zach. Right after prayer was over, it was announced that they had found a pulse. Hearing that, I knew God was moving. All I could do was cry. God is just so good!

Facebook and other friends kept me informed with Zach's progress. After about a week, I was even able to actually text him and talk with him. Adding on to my prior comment, you don't often hear about someone getting struck by lightning—and surviving. Yet Zach did! That's because of the God we serve!

Jesse Glaspell (Zach's cousin)
July 11, 2012—I remember that day very clearly. My cousin, Zach Sandy, came to church camp to hang out. He got there during morning service. After the service, Zach, my other cousins, and I went and played basketball. We had an awesome time together. Later that day, we had a scavenger hunt around the campground. After the scavenger hunt, there was going to be a softball game.

The weather was perfect throughout the day; there was not a cloud in the sky. As Zach and I walked down to the softball field, I was noticing that it started to get a little bit cloudy, but I didn't think anything of it. Once Zach and I got to the field we grabbed a ball and gloves and started tossing to each other. When they picked the teams, Zach and I tried our best to be on the same team. We ended up on separate teams, so Zach went out to left field, and I went up to bat first. It was still a little cloudy, but there were no signs of a thunderstorm or anything like that.

I stepped up to bat, and on the second pitch I got a triple. When I got on base I looked back at Zach, and we started goofing off. The second batter was my other cousin. He swung and missed. Zach and I looked at each other and chuckled good-naturedly. Caleb Tisdale threw a second pitch, and my cousin missed again. I turned around and started talking to Zach. I then turned back and got ready to run. Just before Caleb pitched the ball, I looked back at Zach and smiled one last time. Within at least five seconds of that was when the lightning hit.

The blast knocked a few people, including me, to the ground. I then saw everyone running up the hill to head back to the church. So, I turned around to yell at Zach to come on, and he was lying on the ground stiff as a board. At first I thought he was joking because we had been goofing off all day.

I yelled, "Zach, come on dude! Zach, come on." He wasn't moving at all. Then I saw Caleb running towards him. As soon as Caleb got to Zach, he dropped to Zach's side. I also ran to Zach. All I remember is seeing him with smoke coming off of him and out of him. He smelled like something that had been burnt. As I was standing there, Caleb began performing CPR on Zach.

Pastor Ralph Tisdale and his wife were lying there praying for Zach. I was told to go back up to the gym. As soon as I got to the gym, I began praying.

Later, Sister Tisdale came and asked if we all would get into a big circle, hold hands, and start praying for Zach. Soon my Uncle Bradley and my grandpa came to me and said they were taking Zach to the hospital. They were wondering if I wanted to go with them to the hospital. I went.

We sat at the hospital until Bud and Cheri got there. Later on Zach was taken to Morgantown, and then to Pittsburgh. The following Sunday, after camp was over, my dad, uncle, cousin, and I all went to see Zach in Pittsburgh. I will never forget that day.

Seeing Zach lying on the ground like that was the worst thing I have ever seen. At that point in time, I could tell that my cousin was dead. I thank God for bringing Zach back to life. I also thank Caleb Tisdale for being there and performing CPR on Zach. God is truly amazing! This is an awesome miracle!

Rev. Jim and Liz Curley, Azusa StreetRiders Motorcycle Ministry, Ashland, KY
Zach has greatly affected our personal lives. At the time of the accident we did not actually know Zach. We were good friends with Pastor Doug Joseph, through the Azusa StreetRiders Motorcycle Ministry. Pastor

Joseph sent out a prayer request for Zach, and both my wife and I immediately began to pray. Zach was the subject of constant prayer. We met Zach a few weeks after the accident, at the Azusa StreetRiders National Rally. He immediately made an impact on us with his story.

During the New Year's Eve service of 2012, I had preached that I was ready for G-d to take us to the next level. I was ready to see signs and wonders in 2012. I referred to seeing the sick healed and the dead raised. We immediately started seeing things happen—the sick healed, cancer gone—but the dead raised? I even convinced myself that G-d meant the spiritually dead. But no, He meant the dead. Zach's story proved this.

Through meeting Zach, we saw that every one of these things had happened within the first half of 2012. After meeting Zach, G-d took my faith to a whole new level. I have utilized his testimony many times in my preaching, and it has ministered to many people.

After meeting Zach in Clarksburg, we became friends on Facebook and had several conversations. Some time after the National Rally, we got an email that Zach was to preach at a youth event in Clarksburg at Christian Apostolic Church. My wife and I got on our motorcycle and rode a 400-mile round trip to see Zach preach. The youth at our church had heard his story, and they wanted to meet Zach. So we brought back our picture taken with Zach, and many of our youth have made friends with Zach on Facebook.

Zach has changed the lives of both my wife and me and our church's youth. We have all been inspired. This has proven the power of G-d to us. I am honored to call Zach my friend and brother In Christ. I have now seen signs and wonders, and I have a level of faith that will forever be in my heart.

Britney Gordon

When I heard about Zach it was through Facebook, because I was in Switzerland. As soon as I found out, I had the AYC group and all the other missionaries that were there to pray with me for him. It was amazing to see students from all over the US joined together in prayer for a fellow student whom most had never met. I was so excited when we kept hearing the miraculous news of his recovery. I prayed before my trip that I would see miracles, but I never expected to witness one from thousands of miles away. Zach, I'm so glad that you are doing well, and I can't wait to see what God has in store for you. You are always in my prayers.

Rhonda DeMoss (Zach's aunt)

I remember the day. At first, I thought, "Oh, Zach, you're too young." I was numb, I was devastated. Immediately, I thought of God. A feeling came over me that "Zach is going to be all right." I knew God could work miracles because He had worked a miracle in my life. I sat in front of the computer watching Facebook updates, as family members would post how Zach was. At first the news about Zach seemed grim. It wasn't long until good news started coming. I just sat at the computer, crying tears of joy and saying, "Thank you, Jesus." Friends offered me sympathy because of what happened to Zach, but I would tell them, "Zach is going to be all right." Today, Zach is very much alive. When I go shake hands with him at church, he tweaks my nose instead. It's a joy to see him each day. I give all the glory and praise to God for giving Zach back to us. Zach, I love you. You are special to me.

Cissie Cutlip (Zach's aunt)
I had been praying on June 27, 2012, and talking to God. I remember saying to Him, "We read about all kinds of miracles in the Bible—Lazarus raised from the dead, blind made to see, lame made to walk, deaf made to hear, and so on. God, I want to see those miracles now, right in front of my face." I remember sticking my hand in front of my face as I told God that. I didn't think anymore about it until July 11, 2012.

It started like any other day at our home during the summer. We were chilling. Bethany was watching TV, Jeff was at work, and I was checking out Facebook. At around 2:50 PM, I received a call from my Mom, Verna

Welch. She had just received a call from Nora saying my nephew, Zach, was struck by lightning.

I asked, "Is he OK?" I expected to hear, "Yeah, a few burns, etc. No biggie."

Instead she said, "No, he has no heartbeat right now. He's not responding." She said they were getting things together and heading to Parkersburg to meet Cheri and Bud at Camden Clark Hospital.

Just as calm as I could be, I hung up and said to Bethany, who was in the room beside me, "Zach has been struck by lightning."

She said, "Is he OK?"

I said, "No!" My mind began to race as I tried to think of what to do, who to call or text, or whatever.

I texted these words to Jeff, "Zach's been struck by lightning. He's dead. We can't lose Zach."

He responded back, "We are not going to lose Zach. It will be all right."

I knew we needed to get people praying. I asked Bethany to text Lindsay and Madison at camp and get them praying. Not wanting to alarm any family that might not know yet, or put anything out there for people to think, "Well, he's dead, there's nothing we can do now," I simply sent, "Need prayers for my nephew, Zach. Urgent!!!!"

I remember a few tears falling down my cheeks as I prayed, but I didn't feel alarm, fear, or hopelessness. I felt a calmness take over me. Anyone that knows me knows this is not the norm for me. I usually fall apart.

I got up from my computer chair and walked into the kitchen to get a drink. I stopped right in the middle of my kitchen. If anyone had seen me they would have thought I had lost my mind.

I stuck my left hand out straight and said, "No! No devil! Zach doesn't belong to you! You can't touch him, and you can't do this! I rebuke you! You take your hands off of him right now! He's not yours! He belongs to God!" I then began to thank and praise God for taking care of Zach and for bringing him back to us.

It seemed like forever waiting on that next call. Cheri called me; she was unable to remember whom she had called. I tried to calm her down, and I told her we were praying for her.

I then posted: "Need prayers for my nephew, Zach. There's been an accident." I can't say what time it was (I was more concerned with the news), but it seemed to me like hours. Mom called and said they had a pulse; a strong heartbeat. She indicated they were on the way to the hospital with Zach!

Once I heard that news I posted on Facebook: "OK, here is what's going on. My nephew, Zach, was struck by lightning. He was unresponsive, but now he has a pulse. He is being taken to the hospital. Keep those prayers coming."

I kept praying and kept others praying as we waited for Cheri, Bud, Mom and Dad to arrive at Camden to get more news. About 20 minutes later, I got a call from Mom. They were transporting Zach to Ruby in Morgantown. She wanted to know if I wanted to go with them.

I said, "Yes!" They were halfway to Parkersburg, and they turned around in the middle of the road. I asked Bethany if she wanted to go. She decided to wait and come with Jeff. I got ready, and I drove to Bob Evans to meet them. I jumped in their car and immediately began to ask questions. We prayed, talked and sped to Ruby.

Mom said, "If they pull me over I will tell them where I am going and they can escort me." Hah, hah! Mom said Zach was breathing over top the ventilator machine. That was great news to me! I was so excited. The trip to Ruby seemed very short.

We walked into the emergency room where family and people from their church were waiting. It was hard to sit still and wait for Zach to get there. I will never forget my sister walking through that door with Zach's burnt clothes in a bag in her hand.

She was saying over and over, "Mommy, where's my Mommy?" Mom went to her and they embraced. Cheri gave Mom the bag of clothes to hold. You could smell them through the bag. It smelled like they had been in a fire.

Everyone went outside, gathered in a circle, and prayed. We then waited for Zach to arrive. The ambulance arrived, with Bud in the front. They brought Zach out. We watched from the window as they carried him, with tubes coming from his mouth and nose, into the emergency area and through the double doors. After another wait, the doctor came out to talk with them. They were sending Zach to West Penn Burn Center.

I said, "You people are driving me crazy!" They allowed Cheri and Bud to go back and see Zach while they prepared him to be carried by HealthNet to Pittsburgh. Cheri and Bud, Mom and Dad, and some others went back. Bethany and Jeff arrived, and we waited. They came back out and told me he looked really good.

The hospital chaplain talked with us and comforted us. She was there to pray for us, with us, or whatever we needed. I asked if I could go back and just look at Zach from the hall. I had to see for myself.

As the chaplain walked me back, she said, "They are getting him ready, so we have to stay out of the way." I was fine with that. As I looked at him from the hall I still felt that peace inside me, just as I had been feeling since the first call.

The nurse there asked if they could help me, and I explained I was just wanted to get a look at him. He told me I was welcome to come in, so I did. Zach looked so good. His color was not pale, and I remember thanking God and just praying for Zach.

I told God, "You brought him this far. I know You will do the rest." I don't remember the other exact words I prayed, but I just had that peace that passes all understanding. I knew God was setting us up for the greatest miracle we could see to unfold in front of us!

I leaned over as close as I could get and said, "Zachy, we're going to go get ice cream when you get home. I love you bunches." I walked out of that room knowing God was there and everything was going to be fine. I didn't doubt or fear. I just knew God was in that room. God was with Zach, and the work God started on that ball field was going to be completed in His time, in His way, and for the glory of God.

Once they got Zach prepared for the trip, Mom and Dad, Cheri and Bud, and John prepared to drive to Pittsburgh. Jeff, Bethany, and I came back home. During the ride home, I received a call from a special friend of mine. She was very uplifting and positive. As we talked, I told her I just knew everything was going to be all right.

Mom called to let me know that they were going to slowly take his level of sedation medicine down to see if he was paralyzed or not. I began to send out prayers again. We prayed and trusted God. They indicated he might not know anyone, so I prayed and asked for prayer. I waited the next day for a call. Finally Mom called and told me Zach had tried to get out of bed. He flung his arms and legs. He knew who everyone was, and he talked to them! I was so excited, and I praised God.

They indicated the possibility that his insides were fried and all his internal organs were gone. They were going to run tests to see how bad it was. I began to pray and again sent out a request for prayers. As I prayed for each thing, I thanked God and praised Him for healing Zach and for everything being right. The burns were not even that bad on his body. I still remember how excited we got, praising God as each thing they said could be wrong, or would be wrong, came out with "everything is fine." At one point when I called while they were in with Zach, they put the phone up to Zach's ear.

I said, "Hi, Zachy Doodle."

He said, "Hi."

I asked, "Do you know who this is?"

He said, "Aunt Cissie." I was ecstatic! He knew who I was!

Mom and Dad came home, and we prepared to return on Saturday. I knew that there was a possibility I would not get to see him, but just sitting in the waiting room and being close to him was good enough for me. When we arrived, Zach was sitting there in his wheelchair in the waiting room! I was so excited to see him! He looked at me, and someone asked him if he knew who I was.

He said, "Yes, Aunt Cissie." I ask him what I called him, and he said, "Zachy Doodle." I smiled so big. We chatted, and he kept asking why everyone was there. They told him he had been struck by lightning.

He said, "No, I wasn't." A little later he asked again about what had happened to him.

We told him, "You were struck by lightning."

He said, "Again?" It made us all laugh. Mom told him he had flown in a helicopter.

He looked at his Dad and said, "I did?" Russell told him he had, and Zach said, "Awesome!" It was just great to be with him, to hug him, to look at those blue eyes, to see that smile, and to joke and talk with him. I noticed that when he would stand up really quickly his legs would buckle. I looked down at his legs, and they looked different. I don't really know how to explain it, except that the muscle wasn't as visible as it had been before.

Zach wanted to go back to his room and rest. I took him back and sat with him. He didn't lay still long. He got up, and his legs buckled. We grabbed for him, and he did this little dance.

He said, "I was just showing my cool dance moves." That was Zach, always making you laugh. He is a go-getter, so staying in the bed was not something he wanted to do. He spent a lot of time in the waiting room.

Mom brought his clothes up from that day the lightning struck him, and Cheri was showing them to someone.

Zach got this look on his face, and he said, "Mom, what did you do to my pants? Those are my favorite pants! What did you do to my shirt?" He didn't remember that day, and when he saw the clothes he thought his Mom messed them up in the washer.

When I learned the name of the man who gave him CPR, Caleb Tisdale, I looked him up on Facebook and thanked him for being there that day and doing what he did for Zach—not only CPR, but also praying and seeking the face of God.

Each time we visited Zach, he made us laugh. He enjoyed everyone and tried to make sure he visited with everyone who came to see him. We were able to go and visit him a couple of times in Pittsburgh.

We were excited when they told us he was being moved to HealthSouth after just a week at West Penn. The burns were not that bad, and on to therapy he would go. It was closer for us, so we could see him more there. On the way back to his new room, everyone noticed a sign on the wall that said "Miracle Road." We were told that it was put there for one of the miners from Sago Mines who had been at HealthSouth for rehab. We knew it was no coincidence that Zach was put in that same wing.

We would go up and sit with him during the day while his Mom and Dad had to work. He even got Uncle Jeff to bring him a blizzard from Dairy Queen one day. Just seeing Zach make progress excited me. It was hard to watch him suffer pain from his legs and have no way to help him. We would just sit and pray for him.

Once while visiting, Zach and I were making faces at each other. Zach stuck his tongue out at me.

I said, "Mom did you see what he did?" I told her, and she asked Zach if he stuck his tongue out at me.

He turned to his Mom all serious-looking and said, "Noooooooooooo!"

Before I thought I said, "Liar, liar, pants on fire!"

Without even missing a beat he said, "Is that a lightning joke?" We all burst into laugher.

I looked at Zach's chin, noticed whiskers on it, and I said, "Zach, are those whiskers on your chin?"

He said, "No, the lightning made those prickly things." He was always saying something funny.

One day I was sitting and talking with a lady, Courtney Bayles, about my prayer at my home way back on June 27, when I had asked God to show me miracles before my own eyes. I was just chatting away.

Zach said, "I asked God for three things."

I looked at him, and I asked, "When?"

He said, "At camp. The preacher said, 'Pray for three things, for your church, for your family, and for yourself.' I prayed for growth in our church, for my family to grow closer and spend more time together, and to make me a living testimony."

We all looked at him, and I said, "Well, God answered your prayer that day."

Zach rested very little. He visited with all of us as much as he could. One day when he went to therapy, I wanted to see how well he was doing, so I walked down to the therapy room. I was amazed at how hard he was working his legs to regain strength in them.

Caleb, along with his family, came to see Zach at HealthSouth. I hugged Caleb and his wife and thanked him for helping Zach that day, not only for doing CPR but also for praying and for living in a place where he could touch Heaven right away. Because he lived right, he didn't have to get his life in order first to pray. He was in touch and in tune with God.

I watched as Zach went from a wheelchair to a walker. He would get tired and have Bethany rub his head, and he would fall asleep for a short time. Then up he would be, again chatting with everyone and laughing. He was only at HealthSouth one week, and then home! Zach is a fighter, and he was willing and determined to do whatever it took to go home.

He started rehab and went two times a week. Mom and I, and sometimes Dad, would go with him. Then we would go out to eat. We would sit with him at the house while he slept, just in case he needed something. I would look at his feet and watch each week as he went to therapy. There was a difference in his walk and a change in the way his feet were turned. Each step of progress just made me smile more, and being with Zach and spending time with him made me happy. It reminded me of what God gave us that day.

I would always try to encourage Zach, and usually it ended up with Zach having encouraged me. I had what they called Supraventricular Tachycardia (SVT); my heart would get off beat, and I couldn't get it back. I would end up in the emergency room. I finally decided to get the ablation done so it would not happen again. The night before the procedure, I was scared and Zach sent me a text I will never forget: "God's got this, Aunt Cissie. What He did for me, He will do for you. No worries. He's going to take care of you. I love you." I slept well that night, and when I went for the procedure I told everyone of the miracle God gave us that day, July 11, 2012.

I later learned that a young lady, Lindsay Leasure, from the daycare close to the camp where Zach was, heard about the accident and had her mother, Sandy Leasure, drive her up to the camp. She helped perform CPR on Zach until the ambulance arrived. I thank God for

Lindsay helping that day. I got the opportunity to meet her and her family on August 19. I hugged her and thanked her for being there that day.

The following Saturday we all went to Parkersburg, to the ball field where the miracle started. As I looked out across the field and started walking down the hill, I began to thank and praise God for what He did that day. I thanked Him for bringing Zach back to us.

As I reached his location, Zach said, "Aunt Cissie, see that spot right there? Oh, man, I was gonna make her laugh, but she's already crying." Yet my tears were not for sadness; they were tears of joy. We walked over to the middle of the field, and Zach sat on the ground. I sat beside him.

Zach said, "It is just so peaceful here. I could live here." He laid back, looking at the sky in deep thought. A little boy who had been there that day came up to Zach and told him what he remembered.

The boy said, "You scared me."

Zach said, "I'm so sorry. Where were you when it happened?"

The little boy said, "Batting. Then the lightning hit, and you got hurt, and I never got to bat."

Zach said, "Oh, I'm sorry, man."

The little boy just talked and talked. He was so glad Zach was alive and well. The last time he had seen him it was not a pretty picture. His grandma told me that he cried and cried that day. Just sitting there with Zach meant the world to me, because he was still with us, and we knew God was going to use him for His glory.

Whenever I watch Zach swing, jump, skip, and run, it just makes me smile and say, "That's You, God!" A few weeks ago, Zach said he would race me to the door of the mall. I was excited to see him run so I let him go ahead of me. I watched him run, which was something doctors had said he might never do again. Yet nothing is impossible with God! Never underestimate the power of prayer!

When Zach was little, as we would leave from a restaurant to go to our homes, he would say, "Be careful with your car." As I watched him graduate from high school in May, 2012, I considered that the road ahead would be different than the past 12 years had been for him, with many changes and greater challenges. Never did I think one of those challenges would be a strike of lightning.

Sabrina Martin-Vernon, Congregational Missionary Church
Picture it: July, 2012, a summer afternoon, and I was at the Congregational Missionary Church Camp/Youth Camp. To start, I must give a little backstory for our

situation to show that the events that unfolded were a "God thing." Our camp is usually held at Glenville Recreation Center; however, due to a large storm that came through our area weeks prior, that facility (which we have had booked for that particular week for years) was now unavailable because it was being used as an emergency shelter. So our church was on the hunt to have camp at a new location or cancel it alltogether. To cancel it would mean the disappointment of several youth and adults, not to mention our keynote guest minister, Keith Deltano, a Christian comedian who was to be our minister nightly. Well, just as God worked in getting us Keith, God worked, and we found a camp that was available for the scheduled week. With a lot of extra work and figuring out food preparations and lodging, we were a go. We had a location, speaker, food (and cooks), lodging, and the prayers of many for the unknown of what that week would hold. It turns out we were where we needed to be to allow God to work, to take us out of our comfort zone in more than one way, and put us in the belly of the storm, so to speak. Up until then, God had worked to set the stage as to what was to unfold.

When the news of Zach reached me, I was in the mess hall of camp with every camper, adult worker, and visitor, all just finishing up a snack. We were all fellowshipping around the tables when my mother called me with news of Zach.

She said, "He has been struck by lightning, and they are working to get a pulse." My heart sank, knowing that he, too, was at a church camp. Most of our youth knew him and interacted with him in some capacity. Immediately I hung up the phone, whispered the news to my sister (who was the camp director), and then got the attention of everyone. I asked everyone to please join hands because we needed to pray immediately. That was the burden put on my heart.

As we gathered and held hands, I explained the situation and asked everyone to pray. My sister asked Bekah Goodwin to lead in prayer. What a powerful prayer was prayed! Before long, everyone in the room was crying out for God's mercy and life for Zach. After prayer hearts were heavy, tears were flowing, and Bekah mentioned that God inhabits the praises of His people. So we dropped everything that was on the schedule— not even for a second considering what had been previously scheduled—and we moved straight into praise and worship. We sang, we opened our hearts, we prayed, and we praised God, because only He knew the reason for this tragedy, and He knew the answer.

Afterward, we went back to our normal day. We thought constantly of what had happened. We moved on to our regular vespers service and then to our evening service, where so many realized one never knows what, when, and to whom something tragic will happen.

Wow, what a "God thing" this was! People who had been riding the fence all week and struggling with their own convictions got to hear about something happening that was so profoundly real and heartbreaking. Even if they didn't know Zach, they knew a boy at church camp, just like us, was mortally injured (for all we knew at this point), and it could have easily been one of us. God worked, and hearts were won for Him. Lives were changed from that moment forward with just a phone call.

Just as that first call came in, the second one came, telling that he had a heartbeat and was on his way to the hospital. He had survived! What a praise service we had! We thanked God for hearing the prayers and praises and for setting forth the miracle that only He could do.

Later we learned the rest of the story of what had taken place on scene. It was a week of change for all of us, to step out of our comfort zone and open our eyes and hearts. Zach's accident, as bad as it was, was a blessing. His story blessed our youth and adults, church and community, because we saw the hand and power of God at work that day. All those "God things" leading up to that event gave us the ability to learn. Zach, even in that circumstance and before the whole story was known, was winning hearts to Jesus, opening all the way some heart doors that we had only been able to crack open in the messages we were presenting.

Needless to say, it was a very powerful and awesome camp—the best I have ever seen. God was present *always*, and we were still enough to see and hear it.

"For everything there is a season, a time for every activity under heaven" (Ecclesiastes 3:1 NLT).

"Be still, and know that I am God! I will be honored by every nation. I will be honored throughout the world" (Psalm 46:10 NLT).

Lauren Hulbert, Parma, Ohio

Zach and I first met in 2009. We quickly became friends. We talked endlessly for weeks afterward. Of course, years had passed, and we didn't talk quite as much, but I specifically remember the day I heard about what happened and the events that played out. I just woke up and came into the living room, when my mom had told me what happened. Honestly, I could not believe it. I was completely shocked. Immediately I felt the need to help or to do something. I told all my Facebook friends to start praying. I called my boyfriend and told his family to do the same. I spread the news so more people could hear, and send their prayers in that direction. The response that he received from this was amazing. I was in awe at the miracle I was slowly witnessing. I wish I could have done more, but I just live too far away. I'm ecstatic to see how far he's come along. Zach really is a blessing to all of the people around him.

Jeff Yoho (one of Zach's high school baseball coaches)
Having been around Zach for high school baseball, I
got to know what type of character he had and the way
he carried himself and his faith. When I first heard
about what happened, my first thought was, "How
could that happen to someone like him?" Now I, and
countless others, can see why.

Aaron Regester (friend of the family)
I've known Zach since he was just a boy. I was on the
road when I got a call from my parents telling me what
happened. I couldn't believe that the little blond-haired
happy kid that played basketball with all us big guys
when we were growing up had been struck by lightning
and was in serious condition. I was relieved to hear the
news of Zach regaining consciousness and making a full
recovery. To Zach, Rusty, and the rest of the Sandy
family, I wish you the best.

Lisha Snider Templeton
While I was out shopping, my husband called me. His
brother had called him to say that Zach was struck by
lightning. He had seen it on Facebook. I couldn't wait
to get home to check it out myself. I wanted to know
exactly what happened. I found it on Cissie Cutlip's
post. My heart was so burdened. I prayed all evening,
and when I went to bed that evening, I woke up every
little bit, praying for him. I rose early to check
Facebook for any updates. I followed the story every

chance I got, because it was so exciting to see each update of how he was doing and how things were changing for him for the good. We had the honor of having Zach at the Duck Creek Mission Church to speak of what God has done for him since 7/11/12. Zach, we wish you well in the future that God has planned for you.

Valerie Pittman Keener
Oh, how the Lord has moved for Zach and everyone! His story is very compelling and encouraging in this dark world. It all brought back a memory.... After I began college, I didn't travel as much with Mom and Dad. Yet I remember once getting to go up there to visit you all. Dad had been up there a little while previously without me. He had either prayed for or prophesied over Zach that God really had His hand on him and was going to do something great in his life. Everyone thought that was kind of funny, since young Rusty was the "little preacher" and young Zach was the really active, "rotten little stinker!" They were only maybe five years old and two years old at the time. Do you remember that? God, indeed, had a plan!

Pastor Brad Glaspell, House of the Lord Jesus Christ, Clarksburg, WV
Zach has been my little buddy for years. He loves hunting, and his dad had been bringing him down from time to time to go hunting at our farm. While Zach

was growing up, his parents were pretty protective. Usually they declined whenever they were asked if Zach could stay over with someone or go here or there. So I was pleasantly surprised when they said yes to my request for Zach to come with me for a day at our youth camp. Later, during this dreadful situation, there was a moment when I actually thought, "Why didn't they just say no?"

There were several reasons why I had asked Zach to come. I look up to Zach. I know his life is an example, and I wanted my boys to be around him a little that day. I also wanted him to be around my nephew, Jesse. I had no idea what just picking Zach up that day would end up doing to my family. It was not just a little influence on my kids. Wow! It changed my life as well as many others.

So I headed out to pick him up. We listened to some preaching CDs all the way to his house. Once I arrived to get Zach, Cheri insisted on giving me some money. Zach and I decided to use it for some food from McDonald's. We stopped, got the food, and headed on our way. We were in a big hurry, because we wanted to make it to morning service. At first we didn't talk much because we were eating. Nevertheless, we had about an hour and a half to drive, so after we ate, I put some more preaching on the sound system. By then we were talking a good bit, so the recorded sermon was more of a background. We were just catching bits and pieces of it. The message we listened to was entitled, "Don't Kill My Miracle" by Jerry W. Dillon.

I asked Zach about playing football. Had he thought any more about playing ball in Philippi? He was pretty certain; yes, he loved ball, but he didn't want it to take too much time away from church. He also mentioned that he was feeling a call of God on his life. He wanted to pursue that, and playing ball would make it difficult. I was really amazed while talking to Zach. I thought, "Wow, this kid is really in love with Jesus." By the end of the day I was thinking, "Wow, Jesus is really in love with this kid."

While Zach talked about playing ball since he was little, he talked a lot about JT and how he wanted to be someone that JT could look up to. He said he wanted to make sure JT kept himself on fire for God. He hoped to help JT to not go through some of the trials Zach had faced. He spoke of a time at a high school practice where "friends" were smoking pot, and they offered it to him.

Zach said, "I'm so glad my parents and my pastor had taught me better." When he was faced with that peer pressure, he didn't even have to think about it. "No," was the only answer. He told me how he had seen his friends get involved in all kinds of stuff, yet he had gone to church while other players were getting in extra lifting practice. His coaches wanted him there, and maybe he had lost some favor with the coaches, but he had gained some favor with God. I'm sure glad he did.

The topic changed from football to churches and fellowship. Zach expressed that he was tired of all these divisions between churches and spoke of how we all need to just come together. We discussed the fact that we are in the last days. We spoke of unity and revival.

By the time we got to the youth camp, the church service was just starting. I was thinking, "This is one awesome kid, and he really loves Jesus, and his Ma and Pa." I was really impressed. Surely it was such things that made it really easy for God to heal Zach.

Within just a few hours after our arrival, Zach and Jesse had become the life of the party. This is important for me to point out: here's a kid truly devoted to Jesus, and his coolness factor was way up. The myth says it's uncool to be such a Jesus freak. Zach proved that you could be popular and cool and still be a Jesus freak. By the time I came back to camp, Zach and Jess had a "following" so to speak.

A baseball game was due to start. We were all on the ball field. My sons didn't want to play ball, so I decided to go back to my room. As I was leaving the field, there was a terrifyingly loud *crack*. I literally threw my phone up into the air. Brother Colvin had seen me do it, so he and I were laughing about me being so startled.

As we stood there, kids came running by. Some were saying that a little blond-haired kid had been struck by lightning. I first thought of my boys, and I started towards the field. I then saw Jesse and my boys coming towards me.

I asked, "What happened?"

They said, "It's Zach!"

I said to myself, "Oh, no." As I approached the field, I dialed 911. While I was speaking to the lady dispatcher, I got to where I could see someone starting CPR on Zach. At that time panic kicked in. I hung up, and I began to run. I finally got to where they were gathered around Zach.

Sister Tisdale said, "Do you know him?"

I said, "Yeah, that's Zach, my little 'cuz.'" I began to weep as she hugged me. When I laid eyes on Zach is a moment in time I'll never be able to get out of my mind. Brother Caleb Tisdale was doing CPR. Pastor Ralph Tisdale, Rev. Michael Jadrnicek (the camp evangelist), and I stood there.

I asked whether I should call Zach's parents. The consensus was to just wait a moment. However, after about five minutes of CPR with no response, I was told to call. That was a call I didn't want to make! I hope I never have to make a call like that again. I can't remember all the words I said, but I remember that I had a hard time getting the important words out. Bud, Zach's Dad, understandably became a little frustrated.

Bud said, "What is it, Brad?" I don't remember exactly how I said it, but I remember that Bud was justifiably upset. When I said the words, I felt as though my heart burst. I became sick in my stomach. I felt like screaming until all the air had left my lungs.

We hung up so he could make calls and do what he needed to do. I called my wife, my dad, and a few other people in order to get prayer going. We all knelt down by Zach. Caleb just kept doing CPR. He was like a machine. There was no quit in him. He periodically checked Zach for vitals. There was no response; no breath and no heartbeat.

At some point Brother Nelson showed up, as well as Brother Workman. I was lying on my belly with my head against Zach's head, hugging him. I kept thinking, "Please, God, please. I can't believe this. Lord, please." My prayer life at that moment seemed to be so lacking. Was my walk with God strong enough for something like this? ? Was I ready for such a trial?

Given the situation I didn't think much about taking a picture of Zach at that moment. I now wish I had done it, so I could show just how much God has done for Zach. All natural indications were that death was firm.

As we knelt by Zach, inevitably each face showed worry. We prayed. At times we held hands as we pleaded with God. I cried out, asking why. I never got angry with God, but I did question and was in disbelief.

Half to Caleb and half to God, I begged over and over, "Please, please, please." Pastor Tisdale helped me keep it held together.

The EMS paramedics arrived, and we were kind of moved out of the way at that point. We stood back a little, praying and talking. I supplied the most information to the paramedics, since I was the only one who knew him. The situation didn't look promising. I could see on people's faces that we were starting to lose hope. I was losing hope. I had made a few calls in which I told folks that Zach had been killed. I called Dad and told him Zach had died. I must admit that faith was low at that point.

After the paramedics worked on Zach a while, they placed him into the ambulance. I walked away to check on my kids. The ambulance was soon to be leaving with Zach. Around that time, my dad arrived and got out of his car. I hugged him and wept.

Dad said, "Oh, Brad, this is awful."

I said repeatedly, "He is gone, Dad. He is gone."

Dad said, "Let's drive back down and see what's going to happen; where they are taking him." We did. The ambulance was still rocking as they worked on him. We stood and listened. I heard them discussing whether to give up and call it (referring to calling the time of death). That would have meant letting death become final. By that time, it had been about a half an hour.

To Pastor Tisdale I said, "Oh, this can't happen."

My dad and I pleaded, "Let's pray one more time." We all laid hands on the ambulance.

Within just a few seconds of that prayer, a guy jumped out of the ambulance and said, "We have a pulse."

From that point on, the Lord brought Zach through a healing process. Thank the Lord for all His works and for giving Zach back to us all. Zach has already done a lot with what God has done.

Pastor David Harris Sr., Calvary Apostolic Church, Grafton, WV
I was at Chick-Fil-A working when I heard about Zach. I went to prayer quickly because we know what prayer does. It brings forth miracles, even miracles of people coming back from the dead. Praise the Lord!

Sister Cindy Murphy (Zach's Sunday School teacher),
Christian Apostolic Church
What a privilege it is to know such an awesome God. I
am so thankful. The day I received the call about Zach
having been struck by lightning, my world went into
slow motion. This was one of my Sunday school
students! I cried and prayed. It was like a bad dream,
and waiting for information was agonizing. I finally got
word that he had a faint heartbeat but was not in good
shape. I heard they were on their way to Morgantown.
There was church that night, so I got ready to go. I had
just gotten off Interstate-79, and I was about to turn
onto Route 50. I saw an ambulance on Route 50,
coming from the west.

I thought, "Could this be Zach?" I watched as the
ambulance went past me, entering the ramp to go
northward on Interstate-79, and there inside it was
Brother Bud waving at me! I got so excited that all I
could do was wave and weep. I cried and prayed all the
way to the church. I just knew God was going to do
something great!

As things progressed, hour-by-hour and day-by-day we
watched God's miracle touch. Each week was another
victory. Soon he was home and back to church. We
heard his testimony and watched his recovery.

One thing I know: God is still in the miracle business,
and I will never tire of hearing this testimony. God

bless you, Zach. We are so thankful God chose to let us have you for a while longer to testify of His wonderful miracle power.

Sister Morgan Hurley

Seated on the edge of the VA District Campground's basketball court, I was with Zach's cousins, Brandon Sandy and Samuel Vaughn, when we heard the news. During one of our typical, laughing conversations, Brandon stepped outside to take an urgent phone call from his dad. Minutes later, he came bursting through the doors, sprinting toward Samuel and me. The fear was raw on Brandon's face as he told us that Zach had been struck by lightning. I stared at Brandon, unsure how to respond and praying he had only been joking.

To be honest, the next 20 minutes are a complete whirlwind in my memory. I recall rushing around telling everyone I knew to pray for God to spare Zach's life. I called Zach's girlfriend, Cayla, trying to break the unbearable news. Through tears, I watched Samuel and Brandon shout out prayers in the middle of a lonely football field. Every person attending the youth camp was instructed to report to the chapel, where the youth director explained the situation to everyone. As I heard the words come out of his mouth, the harsh reality hit me square in the face. I'd love to say at that moment I had mountainous faith, but I could only see the storm crashing around me, not the Maker of the wind.

With the roars of prayers around me, I quickly backed out of the sanctuary. I felt like my lungs were caving in as I tried to breathe. I was running toward an unknown destination, endeavoring to escape the truth that surrounded me. My memories of Zach were flooding through my mind too quickly for me to stop them. I didn't realize until that moment what an influence his life had been on mine.

I was so caught up in my thoughts, I hardly realized a young man was speaking to me.

"Did you hear that?" he asked. Then he confidently stated, "The paramedics have a steady heartbeat; your friend is responding!" I nearly collapsed as relief swept over me. My gaze went to the front of the church where hundreds of teens were leaping and praising my glorious, miraculous God.

I could only manage to repeat a few significant words, "Thank you, Jesus."

Greg Bee (helped with Zach's high school baseball team)
I was driving to Pittsburgh when I received the news about Zach. I had spent a lot of time that spring with him and the other baseball players, assisting the coaching staff at R.C. Byrd, and I had a genuine care and pride for each of the young men on the team.

Zach was different. Because he took a lot of pride in his playing, he needed that extra pat on the back, that second reminder to, "Keep your head up, it's just a game." I related well to his love for the game, and I bonded with him over that. Plus, I always tried to keep the team smiling.

Upon hearing the news, I pulled off at the next rest stop and began making phone calls to see if it was true. I was finally able to reach Mr. Sandy personally. I spoke with him multiple times that first day. I wanted him to tell Zach to reach down and keep your head up and fight. Mr. Sandy went on to repeat what I said to Zach in his hospital bed.

After a couple days of not yet knowing the adverse effects of what had happened, I knew I no longer needed to worry when I saw that his dad posted on his Facebook that Zach was moving his feet and had asked for food other than hospital food.

Zach is a fighter and will be his entire life. I know he will be a success.

Elder Keith Fought, Christian Apostolic Church
When Zach's dad called me, I had just dropped my daughter off at work. I could hear in his voice that something was wrong.

Bud told me, "Zach's been struck by lightning, and he is unresponsive. They are taking him to the hospital in Parkersburg."

My first thought was, "This isn't happening. Not Zach." I began to pray as I informed my wife. Soon we were headed to Parkersburg.

Previously, God had prompted me to give "Z" a Thompson chain reference Bible for his graduation, because He was going to use him in a mighty way. So, I felt that Zach just had to survive. At that moment I trusted that Zach was being prepared for what God wanted him to do. I let Zach's mom and dad know what God had shown me.

I told them, "God didn't tell me to give 'Z' that Bible just to let him die!"

Sandra S. Minor (Cheri's co-worker)
It was a beautiful day as I recall. Cheri and I work together, but I was off that day. My sister-in-law, Sheila, was in the store when Russell came to tell Cheri. I do not recall the exact time when Sheila came to my parents' home where I was tending to them. She asked if I had heard the news that Zach had been struck by lightning and it did not sound good for him. All I could do was weep and pray. As I returned to my home, my son, Chris, (a fire chief) asked about his condition. He tried to prepare me for the worst, because he had

dealt with at least two very serious incidents where men had been electrocuted. Hearing about Zach had sickened him.

Later in the day, along with my husband, son, and daughter-in-law, we traveled to Fairmont where my grandchildren were attending a church camp. As we arrived, several came running to us for a report on Zach, as they had received word early on after the strike. They had instantly stopped their activity and formed a prayer circle. They said the Spirit was so real and evident that they knew God was working. Praise His holy name! We returned home late, but I remember waking in the night and falling on my knees to pray and intercede for Zach. No doubt many other faithful believers were doing likewise. I am a very firm believer of Romans 8:28: "And we know that all things work together for good to them that love God, to them who are called according to his purpose." I don't see how anyone could deny that this is a modern-day miracle and that God is using Zach to proclaim His word. My faith has been strengthened, and I give God all the glory. Zach you are a special vessel that God is using in these last days. Thank you for your faithful commitment.

Steve Toompas (Owner, Town & Country Drug Store)
Hearing the agony in a father's voice as he announced the death of a son, and the deafening scream of a

mother acknowledging the loss of a child, empathy took hold as my mind projected my own children into my vision. The father's unforgettable prayer was, "Please, Lord, do not take Zach. Please, please, Lord, take me, not Zach." What if this tragedy was my tragedy, my child gone before me? It was too painful to consider. I cried to myself. Yet there was prayer, prayer, everywhere. So many people prayed, and the prayers were answered. Mercy was granted. Zach lives!

Chera Hurst (Cheri's co-worker)
From 8:00 AM to 4:00 PM I was at my first job. At 4:30 PM I arrived at my second job, at Town & Country Drug Store. I walked in, and the very first thing that happened was Nora grabbed me and led me to the back of the pharmacy.

Nora said, "I have to tell you something important, and do not ask any questions until I am done! Zach was struck by lightning, and it is bad! He was dead, and they now have a pulse. No one knows if he will live. If he does, he could be brain dead." All kinds of things were going through my head by then. I started to weep. I thought, "What a nightmare." I knew Nora would not kid about something that awful, and I could see the seriousness in her face.

We prayed silently all evening, hoping that would help, and it really did. After work I came home and left a message on Cheri's cell phone. I told her I would help in any way with her banking and deposits. Before I finished what I was saying, I began to cry right on Cheri's voicemail service. Cheri called me back later, while she was en route to the hospital. After talking to her for a while, I felt better, because she seemed calmer than I did. We both said, "Love you. Bye." Cheri had asked me to pray for Zach, and I did just that all evening until I went to bed.

Pam Woody

I first heard Zach's story while a patient at HealthSouth Rehabilitation Hospital. The local news told of an 18-year-old boy who had been struck by lightning. I told my husband about it, noting the news said the young man wants to be a minister. Little did I know our paths were about to cross, as Zach was later admitted to HealthSouth in a room just two doors down from mine. I first saw him in the therapy gym, and I spoke to him without realizing who he was. I thought to myself, "What a nice young man." Later, I overheard a conversation about not speaking to the media, and that evening in my room it dawned on me this was the boy that was struck by lightning! We became better acquainted, and I remember being impressed by his faith and the support of his family and friends. Before Zach was discharged, he gave me a turtle his grandma had made with a Life Saver in it and a note that read, "Jesus is a Life Saver." It was such a nice gesture! We exchanged addresses, and since then we have become close with the Sandy family, even having the honor of attending Zach's nineteenth birthday party. It was a wonderful celebration for a remarkable young man!

Renee Talbott (Cheri's co-worker)
I remember the day Zach was struck by lightning. I was off from work. As usual on my day off, I was doing my grocery shopping at Buckhannon Wal-Mart. As I browsed the aisles, my phone rang. It was Brenda from work.

She said, "Did you hear about Zach?"

I asked, "Did I hear what?" She went on to tell me he was struck by lightning. I just couldn't believe it. When I asked if he was OK, she said that she did not know, and that Russell and Cheri had just left the drug store for Parkersburg.

I sent Cheri a text message just telling her that if she needed anything to call, and that I would pray for Zach. I may not be the most religious person, but I do believe in God, and I prayed to Him many times that night to watch over Zach. I went home that day and looked at my son, who is just a year younger than Zach. I hugged him extra tight that day and told him I loved him.

Elder Lorren Godwin (Zach's Youth Pastor), Christian Apostolic Church

On Wednesday, July 11, 2012, I received a phone call from Nora Harris, an employee of Town & Country Drug Store in Stonewood, WV.

Her first words were, "Can you hear that?" I could hear someone crying in the background. It was the sound of someone in deep agony. She said that was Cheri Sandy, with whom my wife and I are close friends.

I asked in panic, "What's wrong?"

She said, "Zach has been struck by lightning and is unresponsive!" I felt like I had been kicked in the stomach.

In addition to them being our neighbors and knowing Cheri through the drug store, the Sandy family attends church with us. They are like family to us. Their boys always make sure my wife has a Mother's Day card, and they are always helping us with the youth and Sunday School. So it felt like someone in my family had died.

I called my wife, and she started calling friends and family for prayer and requesting that they call friends and for them to start praying. I sent an email to our church family and friends stating, "Please pray for Zach Sandy! He has been struck by lightning and is unresponsive. Details are sketchy. Please pray!" In addition, I was on Facebook looking for information. We were getting texts on my cell phone, and emails were coming in wanting details, of which I had none.

While his parents were rushing to Parkersburg to be with Zach, I was trying not to call them, but they got a message to me that they had not been able to contact our pastor, Rev. Doug Joseph, who was in meetings in Charleston, WV. So I tried calling him several times, and I finally got a hold of him on the highway as he was heading home. They immediately headed towards Parkersburg.

In all the confusion of the moment, with poor cell service and too many messages at once, the directions and locations got mixed up. After the Josephs had gone quite a ways on a back road toward Parkersburg, they were rerouted backwards, due to the misunderstanding that Zach was being taken to Charleston. By the time they found out it was Morgantown, not Charleston, they had traveled out of their way almost an hour. So as I was trying to get correct information and relay it to the Josephs, I walked outside to pray.

As I was walking and waiting on texts and calls to confirm information, I began to pray, "Lord I was a pastor for six years, and now a youth pastor almost four years, and I have never yet lost a church member. I am not about to lose one now, like this. *Especially* a young man such as this one, that loves you and serves you as

Zach does. Please do not allow this to happen."
Immediately I got a feeling of peace, letting me know
everything was going to be OK. God was on the scene
and was going to do something amazing!

At almost that moment I got the news, "They have a
heartbeat!" God had once again stepped on the scene
and performed a miracle.

To see Zach today, and to compare him to the way he
was at the first service he attended after the lightning
strike, it is beyond description! God is still alive and
performing miracles! Zach is a living testimony to this!

Jackie Snider (Cheri's co-worker)
How do I begin with this tragic event? It was a normal
Wednesday at Town & Country Drug Store. After I
had finished lunch, I saw Russell get out of his car. He
seemed so upset. He came into my office and told me
Zach had been hit by lightning and to get Cheri. Cheri
came in, and Russell began to tell the story. My heart
just sank as I saw this young couple go numb. They
hugged each other and tried to be strong, and I knew
their faith in God is what held them together.

Russell kept saying, "Please, God, don't take my boy.
Let it be me."

I stood there and prayed, "God please take care of them
and our little boy." At first, I couldn't understand why

God would do this to a wonderful Christian family. I knew we had to get them to where Zach was. I went after Russell's brother to take them to Zach. It was so upsetting to his brother, but God did give him strength to drive them and get them there safely. I prayed all evening hoping that God's will was to spare this wonderful Christian boy and use him for His kingdom.

God spoke to me and said, "In my time, Zach will be fine." I had that wonderful assurance over the next week. We saw God perform a miracle, and our boy was on the road to recovery. Today when I look at him, I see a miracle, and I see a wonderful Christian young man who is spreading the good news. I know God performed a miracle, and I witnessed it in my lifetime.

I was teaching a Sunday school class about miracles, and my 3-year-old granddaughter, Gianna, spoke up and said, "Zach is a miracle." How proud to know my grand kids witnessed God's miracle. Our God is so great, and I know, each day I look at Zach, that he is improving with God's help. I know that God is smiling on him and his family as they spread the good news to the world. I love Zach as if he was my son. Through God, *all* things are possible. We have living proof! Zach Sandy is a true miracle of God and his life is a witness for God each day. He is truly a blessing in my life.

Nora Harris (Cheri's co-worker)
The day that Zach was struck by lightning started out like a normal day. Cheri was telling me about Zach going that morning to a church camp in Parkersburg, because the youth camp he was originally supposed to attend had been canceled. He was excited to go.

Russell had come in once that morning and left. Cheri and I were talking and laughing, when I looked up and saw Russell coming back a while later.

I told Cheri, "There's your husband, and there is something wrong." About that time the phone rang and I answered it. I was trying to listen to what was going on.

I heard Russell say, "Cheri, come here. We need to go to Jackie's office." He told Steve he needed him to come too. I was still on the phone. He looked at me and said, "Nora, now." I had never heard Russell speak like that before. He is a very quiet man. I knew something was really wrong. I put the phone down and rushed into Jackie's office.

By the time I walked in, Cheri was screaming, "Please don't take my baby."

Russell was crying, "Take me, not my son." I asked what was going on. As they told me, I was thinking, "This can't be." You hear about these things happening to other people, not someone you know. We were trying to pray and comfort Cheri and Russell. That is one great thing about working at Town & Country; we all pull together when someone is hurting. There was a lot of praying and crying.

I asked Cheri, "Who do you want me to call first?" She wanted me to call her dad & mom. I called and told her dad what had happened and that Cheri needed them. I tried calling her pastor and couldn't get a hold of him, so we called Muffin (that's an affectionate nickname a lot of church folks and friends use for Lorren Godwin, the youth pastor at Russell and Cheri's church). Then I went outside looking for Russell to check on him. Someone was on the phone for him. I think he went outside so Cheri wouldn't see how upset he was.

We decided that Russell's brother, John, would drive them to Parkersburg. Russell and Cheri were in no condition to drive. Jackie went to get John. He came down, and we got them out the door and into his car. After they left, it was eerie how quiet it became. We could hardly stay focused; a part of us went with them. I kept thinking that if Zach didn't make it, what would happen to them? They are a very close-knit family. Yet in my heart, I kept saying, "God is bigger than this. He can pull Zach through this." This incident has changed this family. They have gotten closer, stronger, and more grounded in the Lord. We went to hear Zach preach the other night, and what a message! God is using Zach in a mighty way. My husband and I went over to the fellowship hall afterwards, and my husband told Russell how much he changed because he was so quiet. Russell and Cheri both have a beautiful testimony. God is using this family.

JT Sandy "#14" (Zach's cousin)
On July 11, 2012, I was with my Mamaw and my cousin, Landon. We were all sitting on the couch watching TV. Suddenly my Uncle Ashley came into the house. He went straight to the TV and turned it off. He told Landon and me to go to Landon's room. Once we were in the room and the door was closed, we heard my Mamaw begin to wail. Landon wanted to go see what was going on. I worriedly walked out to see what happened. My Mamaw's face was full of tears.

Uncle Ashley looked at me and said, "Zach was in an accident."

I ran to grab Mamaw's phone to call my Dad. His phone was busy, so I called my Aunt Cheri. She answered.

I begged her in a frightened voice, "Please, please tell me it isn't true."

She said, "Here, talk to your Dad." I asked Dad what had happened, and the next few words that came over the phone shocked me.

He said, "Zach was struck by lightning." Then he said, "Zach has a pulse, and they are rushing to the hospital. Pray!" I went back to the living room and prayed with my family. At that moment, I did not realize that my Mamaw was still unaware Zach had been struck by lightning.

Instantly, the door flew open again. It was my Aunt Linda. She came in with eyes full of tears and joined in praying. After some time, Linda told Mamaw what actually happened, Mamaw flipped out even more. We got the news that Zach had been playing softball at camp, and had been dead for over 25 minutes. We received pictures of Zach's clothes and shoes.

The reason I was so worried and scared at the time was Zach isn't just a cousin to me. He is like a brother to me. Zach was the one who went to the backyard and practiced with me on baseball, basketball, and mostly football.

Zach was and still is my role model.

Note: JT always desires to come and spend the night with Zach. JT requests #14 from his coaches because that was Zach's number. Be sure to read Brad Glaspell's foregoing testimonial for Zach's feelings about JT.

Mark & Meredith McClain, Christian Apostolic Church
Being that Zach's journey had started about an hour
before his birth, Meredith and I were there on the
ambulance that day, not knowing who the patient was
or what we were actually getting into when the 911 call
came into the station. We had heard the address and
initial description. Through the wisdom of experience,
we already gathered that it was going to be a rough call.
After fully realizing the seriousness of the situation, we
did not waste any time on scene. The baby that was
about to be born was in distress, with a prolapsed cord
extruding. There was heavy, uncontrollable bleeding.
After arriving at the hospital, Cheri was immediately
taken to the operating room.

Afterward we heard that the child was born and was
doing well. As the years progressed, Meredith and I
became closer to Russell and Cheri. When Meredith
and I finally started coming to church, we rediscovered
that little boy from years before, the one that was
almost not born. Over time, God started to deal with
me about my walk with Him. He began using me to
give words of encouragement or direction for some. I
take no credit for anything. It was God who was
speaking through me.

About two months before Zach's lightning strike, I was
at the altar at our church, praying for those that were up
front. As I knelt down beside Zach, God revealed to
me that Zach had a desire to be used by the Lord and

that he was about to be sent by God on a journey like no other. As I spoke these words of encouragement to Zach, I advised him to prepare for what Gad was about to do in his life. I then turned and saw his mother standing halfway back in the church.

I approached her with tears in my eyes and said, "God is about ready to use Zach. Be ready to let him go when that time comes." This would come at God's time, not our time. (At that time, the devil was trying to create turmoil in Zach's family.)

After hearing the news of Zach having been struck down by lightning, I said to myself aloud, "It has happened." I was concerned that if this family was not strong enough to withstand this incident and truly trust in God with their whole hearts, it would be the end of this family's spiritual walk. After hearing that people were on their way to Morgantown to pray for him, I had expected to see the usual amount of people gathered around, but wow, what a sight to see! There was a very large crowd of people outside, near the ambulance, praying with their hands lifted toward heaven. When I saw that, I knew Zach would recover. Where else have you seen that many people praying in public with such sincerity, not caring what onlookers thought about them raising their hands to God, lifting their voices in intercessory prayer, speaking with tongues—on a parking lot? Those were Apostolic Pentecostal folks! I'll let you think on that.

Zach, God has plans for you. Never let anybody tell you any different, whether they like it or not. Yes, I know that Zach Sandy doesn't want to draw attention to himself, but regardless, listen to God and always do what He says. Zach, you will have people come up to you unexpectedly and ask you to pray for them. Pray and exercise faith. Tell them, "Your faith has made you whole." Some people just need a little faith for their healing. Don't ever be afraid or hesitate to pray for people, because it may be their last time to have an opportunity to pray.

Where much is given, much will be required (see Luke 12:48). We are living in different times. This is a day and age where God is going to pour out His Spirit like never before! Some will not accept it and make mockery of us, but don't be offended, for it is God they are laughing at.

In Leviticus 11:44-45, God told His people, "Sanctify yourselves, and ye shall be holy." The more holy you remain and the more you sacrifice, the more God will use you and reveal things, showing that ultimately God is in control over all things.

Cheryl Colombo, Christian Apostolic Church
Tiffany Sandy (Zach's cousin) and my daughter, Madison, are best friends. Tiffany's birthday just so happens to be on July 11. We had decided to make cake pops for her party. They're fun. They're simple. They're

easy. However, my maiden name is Murphy, and there is an epigram known as Murphy's Law, "Anything that can go wrong, will go wrong." Well, my cake pops were not turning out. What once was considered to be a savory birthday delight had turned into a disaster of epic proportions. I advised Madison to call Tiffany and tell her we would be late. About an hour passed before we were able to make our way towards Nutter Fort. Soon we were passing the pharmacy where Cheri Sandy works.

The phone rang.

Bud Sandy was on the other end. There are no real words to describe *that* tone in his voice. All that you could assimilate was that something was wrong. Something was *very* wrong.

"Where are you?" he asked quickly. "You need to come here. Zach has been struck by lightning, and there is no pulse. We need you."

I zoomed into the parking lot of the pharmacy and put the car in park. I looked over at Madison and explained what was happening. She immediately began to break down into tears.

I said, "We can't cry, Madison. Pray." I felt like I was running, but couldn't get to Cheri fast enough. Bud was pacing outside, talking on his cell phone. He was distraught, waiting for any new information coming to his ears. I walked in and saw Cheri, hysterical beyond words. Fighting fear and terror, I grabbed Cheri and began to pray. A few words passed through my mind:

Save him.

Have mercy.

Miracle.

I looked to find Bud, and he said, "The ambulance is surrounded by people praying. They found a pulse." John Sandy showed up, seemingly immediately after Bud had said those words, and they took off for Parkersburg.

We arrived at Tiffany's house. Instead of a party atmosphere, the mood was solemn and subdued. As the group gathered, I saw familiar faces. Felicia, Nathan, Chelsi, Tiffany, and, of course, my own daughter, Madison. This could have been any one of them. Lightning happens 40 to 50 times per second worldwide. There are an estimated one and a half billion (1,500,000,000) lightning strikes per year. As these people gathered, the severity of this life-altering event began to soak in. We joined hands in prayer.

Tracy (Zach's aunt) made plans to go to Parkersburg, and Madison and I left for home. I got another phone call. I had to pull over again. Tears streamed down my face as I told Madison. The doctors were saying Zach's internal organs could be damaged beyond repair, and there was no way to know yet if there was brain damage and if so, how much. We continued to pray the entire way home for mercy and a miracle. I was late for a birthday party for my daughter's best friend. I ruined an entire batch of cake pops. I wasn't late for a miracle.

Bethany Cutlip (Zach's cousin)
What if? What if one day your whole life just changed? What if something happened that turned your whole world upside down? Life is taken for granted way too often. Life seems so simple, but it can change in an instant. Something as quick as a flash of lightning could change your whole perspective on life.

July 11, 2012—just another day, right? Wrong. The day started off as a typical summer day for me. I got out of my bed, did my normal daily routine, and got dressed. My mom and I did a few things throughout the day. I was watching a movie in my mom and dad's room (the only room with a television). I was about halfway through the movie when the phone rang. I thought it was just another phone call; I couldn't have been more wrong. My mom hung up the phone and yelled into the room. I put the movie on pause so I could hear her.

With a voice as calm as the summer breeze, my mom proceeded to say the words, "Zach just got struck with lightning." I could not believe it. My cousin, Zach

Sandy, struck by lightning. The way she said it sounded like he was possibly all right. When I asked, my mom burst into tears as she said a word that hit me like a speeding bullet. That word was, "No."

You can imagine how upset I was. I ran into my room with tears streaming down my face. I immediately started praying. All I could say was, "No, God, no. We can't lose Zach. He can't die!" As soon as I got myself calmed down, I grabbed my phone. My best friends, Lindsay and Madison Beverlin, who were at church camp, knew Zach well, too. As fast as my fingers would allow me, I texted them. I alerted them of the situation and asked them to stand in for prayer for Zach that night at service. At this point my mom had already started a prayer chain of her own, and the word was spreading fast. All that was left was prayer.

My mother and I sat and waited for further news. I finished my movie before the next call came. Zach had a pulse and they were headed to the hospital. I began to thank Jesus for saving my cousin. In the weeks to come, we visited Zach at Ruby, West Penn, and HealthSouth. As you can see, life is unpredictable. We are not guaranteed our next breath, let alone our next day. I know that God had a plan to use Zach in ways that only God could. I will never take life for granted again because of that day, and I will always give God the praise!

Brian Murphy Jr, Christian Apostolic Church

Zach has always been a strong follower of God. I have always known that. I grew up with him and the church family for the most part. We would see each other at church, until my dad, Brian Sr., started going to Calvary Apostolic Church in Grafton, WV; then we saw each other every once in a while during visits we would make to his church and vice versa. I somehow drifted away from church through my middle school and high school years. I wasn't necessarily living the "Christian lifestyle." So when I heard about Zach getting hit by lightning, it wasn't an impact on my life immediately. I was shocked, of course, and to think it happened at church camp! That just doesn't happen. Still, I kind of just shrugged it off to the side. "Ya know, eh, big deal," I thought. I went on, remaining out of church.

September came around. God gave me a wake up call. On the 14th, I straightened out my choices big time, but I still wasn't serving God. After all that, I got a girlfriend who was not in church, so I still wasn't there yet. Well, the time came when we broke up.

I called my dad and said, "I just feel like nothing is going my way." I listed several situations I was battling. Finally I asked him, "Can I come over to your house?" If you all know my dad, you know it shouldn't have even been a question.

He said, "Of course, Bub!" It just so happened that it was the Saturday during his church's revival week. I went on Saturday and Sunday, and Brother Donnie Harris' sermons really pointed right at me. Then on March 18, I reviewed a random text message that said, "Hey, is this Brian Jr?" Later he told me it was Zach.

Zach invited me to Wednesday night service at Christian Apostolic Church, right after the revival in Grafton. Let me tell you, Sunday services are not the only time God can let loose in the church! I prayed through that night and received the Holy Ghost once more! I am now serving the Lord faithfully, and now I am living the "Christian life." See, I don't really get my inspiration from Zach just because of his miracle. My inspiration comes from the fact that this is a guy that is my age who has stayed faithful. This is someone I grew up with (we both went to public school, him to R.C.B., me to Bridgeport) and yet when I took the wrong path, he stayed on the right one. *That* is what I look up to. Now, because of a text, not only from Zach—now my best friend and my brother—but also with help from Jesus... I am *redeemed!*

Jenni Claypool, Christian Apostolic Church
My family and I were visiting my parents in Ohio. We had just gone into the grocery store to grab a few things when my phone rang, and I saw it was Cheri. My first thought was to call her back later when we were done.

I remember saying to myself, "No, I need to get this call. She needs something." I was not prepared for what she told me. Cheri broke out with a cry that no mother wants to hear.

She said, "Zach got hit by lightning." Her cry said a million words. I felt speechless, so I handed the phone to my husband, Baron. He got all the information that he could and told Cheri we would pray and contact everyone we could to pray.

When Baron got off the phone with her, I looked at him and just said, "Zach is fighting for his life this very moment." We all began to pray right there in the store. This was not something that could wait until we got into our car or back where we were staying. Every second mattered.

After we finished praying we couldn't even check out. We left our cart there with everything in it and went to the car. We began contacting everyone we could to call on the name of Jesus for Zach and his family. I remember between phone calls I would look in the back seat and see my daughter, Alanna, crying out to God.

I remember praying, "Jesus, this is too much for anyone to handle." We knew a miracle had to come!

We started towards Parkersburg, which was about a four-hour drive. About 15 minutes after we left, we were questioning whether or not we should go. All we knew was Zach had a pulse. I started to feel uneasy about going, and that feeling was getting stronger. I told my husband I really felt we needed to turn around. As much as we all wanted to be there, we knew no matter where we were, the best thing we could do was to keep praying. We later found out the hospital Zach was supposedly going to changed several times. We would have gone so far out of our way in each direction that we would have never made it to Zach that night.

We found out he was going to be at the West Penn Burn Center in Pittsburgh, which was only two hours away, so we were able to go see him the next day. We are so thankful God kept His hand upon Zach. Miracles do happen!

Elder Baron Claypool, Christian Apostolic Church
My wife, Jenni, my daughter, Alanna, and I were visiting my wife's family in Brunswick, a suburb of Cleveland, Ohio. We were shopping in a grocery/outlet store when Sister Cheri Sandy called Jenni's cell phone. I listened and tried to ascertain what the situation was, because I could see the change in Jenni's expression. Jenni spoke to Sister Cheri for a brief moment, and then she handed me the phone.

She said, "Zach was struck by lightning." I spoke with Sister Cheri. She advised me that Brother Zach had been struck by lightning, and he was without pulse or respiration. I was only on the phone with her for a moment, but I will never forget the sound of fear and anguish in her voice. I gathered a few details and disconnected the call.

Jenni said, "Zach's fighting for his life right now." I handed the phone to my wife, and immediately Alanna and I went to our knees. We all began praying, calling on the name of Jesus in front of all the customers and employees. We left the items we had selected in the cart and got into our car. We went back to my in-laws. We were constantly updated on Brother Zach's condition, and we continued to pray. Thank God for His wonderful, miraculous power, which He demonstrated and continues to demonstrate in Brother Zach's life! To God be the glory!

Tiffany Sandy (Zach's cousin)
On July 11, 2012, my cousin, Zachary Sandy, was struck by lightning. It was also my birthday that very day. My boyfriend, Nathan Martin, and I were sitting on my couch, when I got a phone call from Jesse Glaspell. He was there with Zach at the time.

He said, "Tiffany! Zach was struck by lightning, and I can't get a hold of his parents. I don't know what to do!" Knowing the jokester that Jesse is, I didn't believe it at first. Then he went on saying, "I'm serious," so I told him I would try to get the message to them.

Almost as soon as we hung up, a lady from Town &
Country Drug Store knocked at the door.

She said, "They want your dad." I woke him up and
told him that Zach was struck by lightning, and they
were asking for him. My Dad got up so very fast, threw
on some clothes, and ran out to meet Bud and Cheri.
When he left, I went to go to my Grandma's, but then
I remembered she was in Georgia. I knelt down on her
porch, and I prayed. As I was praying, Cheryl Colombo
arrived with Madison Colombo and Chelsi Levier.
Then came my Aunt Susan with Rachel and Shawn.
Then my sister, Felicia, and my Mom came home.

We all gathered in a circle at my house and prayed with
faith. We knew that since God had brought Zach back
to life, He was surely going to do more! A few of us
went and packed clothes for Zach and his parents.
Then we headed to Morgantown. When we got there,
the waiting room was completely filled with people, all
there because of Zach. Everyone that could be there,
was there. We all waited for several hours before they
sent Zach to the Burn Center in Pittsburgh. My
parents and many family members went there with him,
but I was sent back home. I didn't get to see him until
the second week, when he was brought to the Rehab
Center in Morgantown.

This all raised my faith higher than it has ever been! I
had heard of wonderful miracles, and they touch me as

well, but it is so different seeing this and experiencing it in your own family. It has put our church on a high.

Greg and Tiffany Hoskins, Christian Apostolic Church
It was a hot, humid day in Lewis County, WV, with storm clouds in the sky on Wednesday the 11th day of July, 2012. At that time, I was working day shift for the Lewis County Sheriff's office. I was patrolling US Route 19 just south of Weston, and I had just driven under the Interstate-79 overpass at exit 91. My phone rang out. I looked at the screen, and it said Bro. Bud Sandy. I thought perhaps Bro. Bud was calling to talk about "whatever." Our conversations are always a pleasure. So I answered the phone.

Bro. Bud said in a very stressed-shaken voice, "Hey brother, please, please pray for Zach. He was struck by lightning. Pray right now, please."

He said that they were on their way to West Virginia University's Ruby Memorial Hospital, and Zach was being transported by ambulance. (Perhaps this was because the weather was not fit for HealthNet to fly?) So I told Brother Bud that I would be in prayer just as soon as we got off the phone. For the next two to three hours, I prayed while I drove throughout the county. After prayer, I felt a peace come upon me, and I knew that the Lord would see Zach through this trial that he was facing. When I got home from work, my wife, Tiffany, and I were determined to go to WVU Ruby

Memorial Hospital to show our support, along with other church families, and bind together in fervent prayer for God to touch Zach's body.

Zach, we then began to receive updates about your status. When we would receive this information about certain physical concerns, we would bind together and pray for that specific need in your body. All of those who joined in prayer at Ruby Hospital were outside, just beyond the doors to the emergency room, standing in a circle. Some were holding hands, and some had their hands raised high. Tears were running down many faces. We were not shy about our prayers, nor quiet with our voices. The Lord heard us that day; there's no doubt in my mind. I'm sure that there were many people who saw and heard God's people in prayer. In the midst of fervent prayer, I began to intercede along with many others. God moved mightily, and He again gave me a peace in my soul about what He was doing. According to reports, you were in stable condition and you were going to be flown to the West Penn Burn Center in Pittsburgh, PA.

A few days later, Tiffany and I came up to the West Penn Burn center to visit with you and show our support for you and your family. At this point God began the healing and ministry for you. Wow, what a testimony! When we arrived, we met up with your mom and your aunt, Tracy Sandy.

We were in the waiting room, and your dad came over to me and said, "Come on, Reverend Hoskins and wife. Let's go."

I said, "Where are we going?"

He answered, "To see Zach."

So your dad, Tiffany, and I walked back to your room. Tiffany and I brought a WVU digital camo hat for you. I was glad that we were able to bring the hat to you ourselves.

I was nervous and didn't know what to expect. As soon as we walked into the room, you immediately recognized Tiffany and me. We gave you the hat, and you liked it and put it on. You kept telling the nurse you were ready to go home.

At one point I became overwhelmed with everything that was going on. I became lightheaded and almost passed out. I guess for me, when I see someone that I care about in distress, it affects me differently than when I see someone at work whom I don't know. I was OK, and the staff there offered me a coke and snack. It took me a good half an hour before I was back to normal. Shortly afterward, we all went out to eat.

We then came to visit you at HealthSouth in Morgantown. It was so awesome how the Lord brought you through this trial, and I'm glad that God has

allowed you to minister to so many people about what
He has done for you and what He can do for them.
Tiffany and I love you, buddy. We're so proud of how
you have allowed God to use you, yielding to His will.
We're all so very glad that the Lord brought you back
to us that day. You are a true miracle, and I'm so
thankful I still have you to call my little brother. We
love you.

Pastor Doug and Sister LaDonna Joseph,
Christian Apostolic Church, Clarksburg, WV

This precious Sandy family reminds us of Job. God
allowed your entire world to be shaken to the core, and
still you trusted in Him. Elder Zach, we salute you and
admire you for your patience, tolerance, faith, and
determination! As Brother Jeff Arnold observed, hell
cannot stop a worshipper! You, my friend, are a true
worshipper who worships the Father in Spirit and in
truth. If the Lord tarries, five years from now, and at 10
years, and at 50 years into the future, we'll still be
discovering the impact of this incident on the souls of
men and women. Yet truthfully, only in eternity will we
gain the fullness of perspective on all the hundreds of
thousands of reasons—souls—why God chose to
permit this tragedy, so that He could bring about this
triumph. Your wise father summed it up well in the
twelfth chapter of this great book. May God help us all
to gain and keep a right perspective regardless of what
trials and tragedies we face. Zach, you're a true hero!